Monica Galetti

THE SKILLS

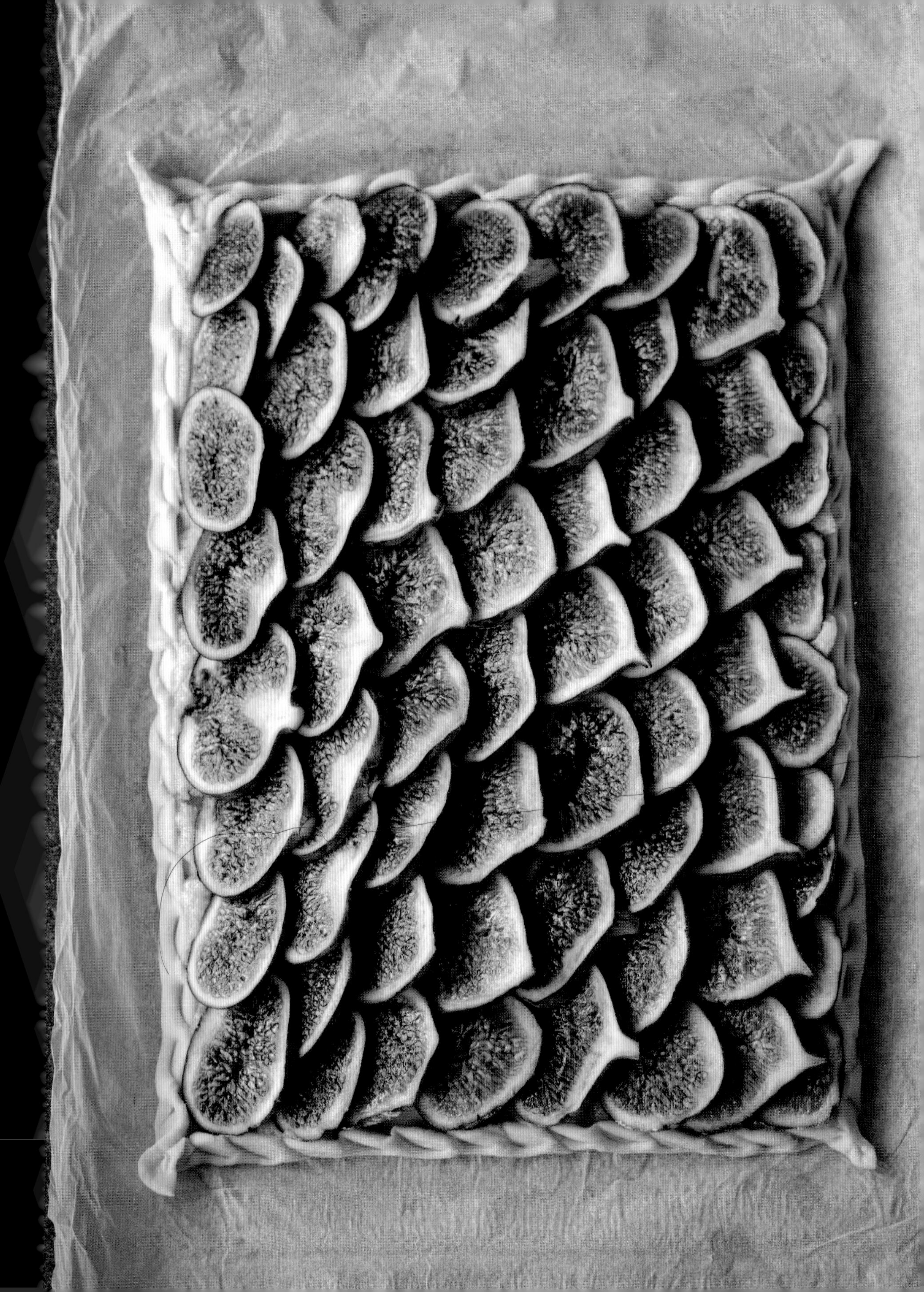

Monica Galetti

THE SKILLS

How to become an expert chef in your own kitchen:
120 RECIPES, TIPS AND TECHNIQUES

Photography by Cristian Barnett

quadrille

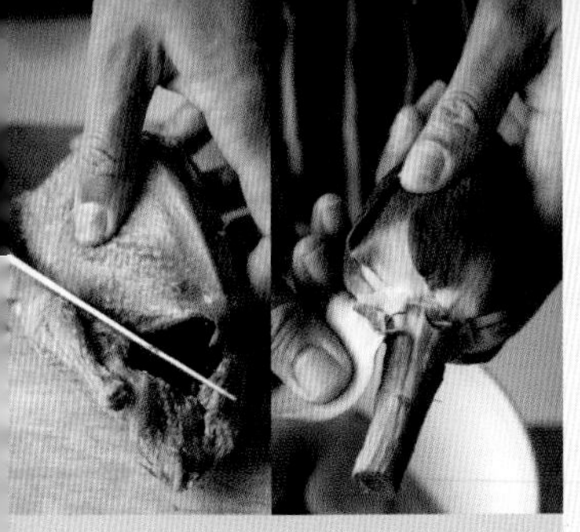

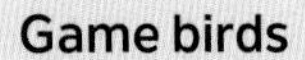

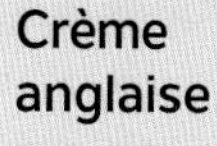

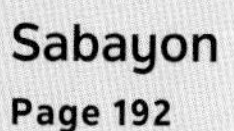

Foreword

I have known Monica for a number of years now and I'm honoured to call her a friend. She wears her heart on her sleeve and cooks with desire and soul. Every time Monica puts something in a pan or in the oven, you can feel that it is done with love. Many chefs have this ability to cook the food that they want to eat, but not many are able to do it with such consistency, warmth and passion. She creates food with flavour that we all want to eat. This is a skill that you cannot teach; it is one that is inbuilt, but when you mix that with her rock-solid classic foundation and training from the great Michel Roux Junior, this makes for an incredible force of flavour. If you have been lucky enough to eat Monica's cooking, you will know exactly what I mean.

Monica Galetti is arguably one of the greatest chefs cooking in the UK today and in this book she shares with you an insight into her skillset, technique and understanding. The book will lift the basic cook to a great one, help teach young chefs in training, or remind old dogs like me of techniques that we quite often take for granted – from prepping artichokes to filleting fish or honing your butchery craftsmanship. After reading this book, you can only come away inspired, enthused and with a commitment to improve the food in your life. We can all learn a thing or two from Monica whether it be juggling family life, being able to cook at the highest level or just a desire to succeed.

Monica's book, and she as a person, are an inspiration to all of us.

Tom Kerridge

Introduction

I often find that home cooks are so daunted by certain kitchen skills that they imagine they'll never be able to master them. They will avoid buying fresh squid, for example, because the thought of preparing it and knowing how to handle it is just too frightening. Only a chef can have this sort of technical skill, right? Making puff pastry yourself must surely be impossible if you're not a pastry chef... But the truth is that anyone can do these things with the right instructions and support. It's usually much easier than people think, and of course the more you practise, the easier and quicker it gets.

In this book, I've chosen the 20 key skills that I think are the most useful to master and the most versatile in terms of the recipes that you can make from them. None of them are difficult – I promise! There are so many benefits to learning these techniques: as well as turning out endless amazing recipes based around them, you can potentially start on all sorts of other culinary adventures. We all know that if we buy a whole chicken and joint it ourselves, we save money (it's much more economical to buy the whole bird than pre-prepared parts of it). Additionally, though, we have the carcass and bones with which to make brilliant stock. Even the skin from a pork belly that you've butchered at home can be made use of in the most delicious little puffed pork-skin crisps (page 45). And once you've made traditional frangipane (pages 182–183), you can experiment with other types of nut to make a whole host of desserts.

I would love to be able to show you in person how to carry out these skills, but the next best thing is to show you through step-by-step pictures of me in my own kitchen. There's no better way to understand how to fillet a fish or judge the correct consistency of mayonnaise than by seeing it done in front of you. I hope the photographs will give you the guidance and reassurance you need, as you stand at your kitchen counter, to follow through and master each skill. Don't be disheartened if you make a few mistakes along the way, or if your lamb saddle looks a bit lopsided the first time you attempt to roll it up. You will improve every time.

When you try some of the recipes in the book, I hope you'll realise how feasible it is to make restaurant-standard food at home if you just have the right building blocks. There's nothing more rewarding than serving plates of mouth-watering food to your dinner guests and then hearing their appreciation when they tuck in. You'll gain confidence (and admirers!) so quickly and you'll start to feel like you can put your own twists on the recipes, or try your very own creations. There's no end to the dishes you can produce with these invaluable skills.

I hope you'll feel inspired to get your apron on and your hands dirty, and to splatter the pages of this book over the years with your first hollandaise or that truly melt-in-the-mouth risotto you've always hoped to perfect. Good luck, and enjoy!

Monica

RECIPE NOTES

Use organic or free-range eggs.

1 large egg yolk weighs about 20g and 1 large egg white weighs about 40g. It is best to weigh egg yolks and whites as stated in the recipe; numbers of yolks and whites are given as guidelines only and will vary from egg to egg.

Buy unwaxed fruit if you are using the zest.

Use fresh herbs unless otherwise stated.

Baby artichokes

1 Prepare some acidulated water by filling a bowl with water and adding some vinegar or a couple of slices of lemon, and a pinch of coarse sea salt.

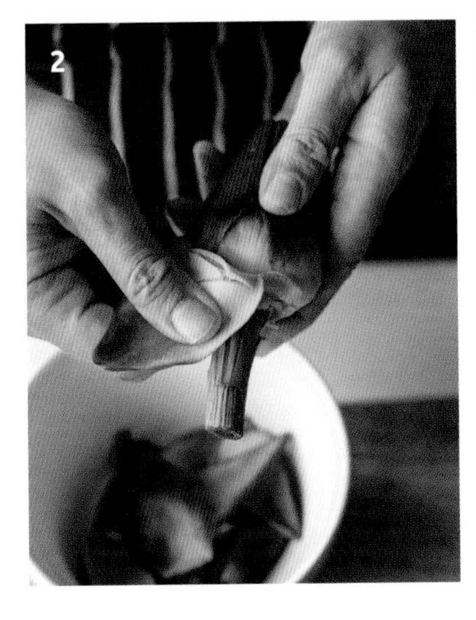

2 Peel off and discard the first 2–3 layers of outer leaves. Cut the end off the artichoke stalk with a small, sharp knife.

3 Cut off the top half or two-thirds of the artichoke.

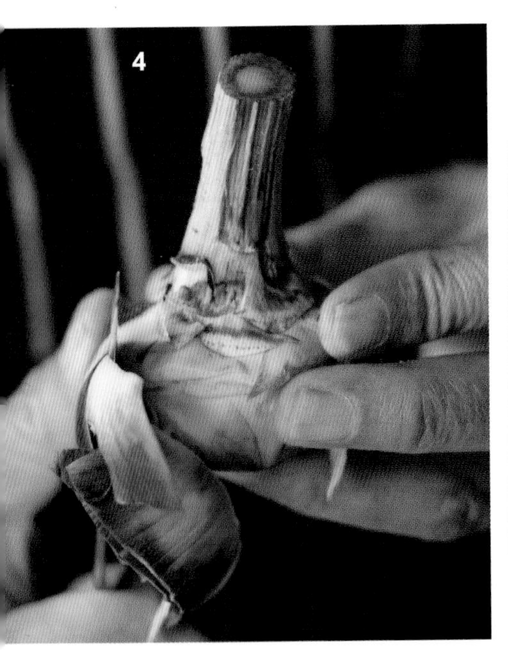

4 Cut away the remaining, tough leaves at the base of the artichoke. Using a teaspoon or melon scoop, scrape out the hairy choke inside the heart of the artichoke.

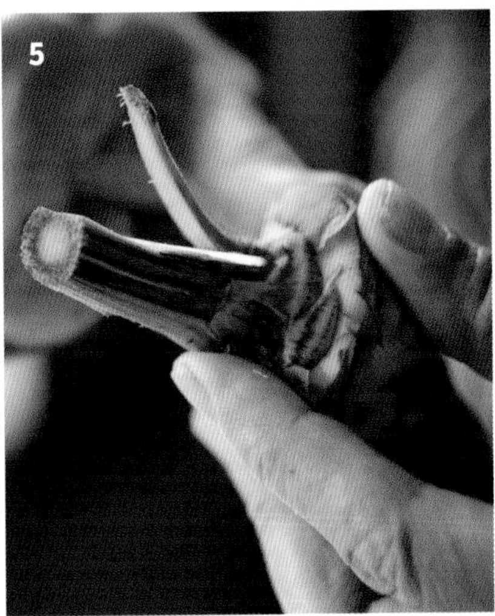

5 Using the same knife or a vegetable peeler, peel the stalk to you reveal the lighter part.

6 Place the prepared artichoke in the bowl of acidulated water until ready to use.

SERVES 8–10

8 globe artichokes
Vegetable oil, for cooking
2 banana shallots, thinly sliced
6 slices of Bayonne ham
2 tbsp sherry vinegar
1 tsp honey
2 tbsp rapeseed oil
200g mature Cheddar, such as
3 year reserve Davidstow Cheddar
1 tbsp chopped flat-leaf parsley
Juice of 1 lemon
Sea salt

Artichokes with Bayonne ham and aged Cheddar

Prepare the artichokes (see opposite) and cut lengthways into slices the thickness of a pound coin. Heat a plancha or a griddle pan on high, add a small amount of vegetable oil, then add the artichokes and shallots to colour. Season with salt and cook for 2 minutes until just tender.

Remove and add the ham, cooking until just crisp.

Whisk the sherry vinegar, honey and rapeseed oil together and use to dress the artichokes and shallots. Put into a serving bowl and top with the ham. Shave the Cheddar over the top and sprinkle with the parsley and lemon juice to serve.

Note: When preparing larger artichokes, like globe, the stalk should be snapped off and discarded. When the top half to two-thirds of the artichoke is cut off, you should be able to see the small, thin, yellow or purple leaves that are tightly packed at the centre of the artichoke. Pull some of these out until you reveal the hairy choke underneath. Scrape and scoop out all of this choke until hollow.

SERVES 4

4 globe artichokes
Olive oil, for cooking
1 garlic clove, peeled
1 small baguette, very thinly sliced
1 large fennel bulb, with fronds reserved
10g baby spinach
10g rocket or dandelion leaves
1 tbsp chive batons
1 tbsp flat-leaf parsley leaves
1 tbsp tarragon leaves
10 pickled walnuts, roughly chopped
1 small preserved lemon,
seeds removed, skin finely sliced,
and flesh roughly chopped
2 walnuts, to garnish
Sea salt and freshly ground black pepper

DRESSING

100ml walnut oil
1 tsp Dijon mustard
2 tbsp white balsamic vinegar

Artichoke salad with lemon and fennel

Prepare the artichokes (see page 10 and Note on page 11) and set aside in a bowl of acidulated water.

Heat a little olive oil with the garlic clove in a frying pan and cook the baguette slices on both sides until golden, then drain on kitchen paper.

Thinly slice the fennel, using a mandolin, and place in a bowl of iced water. Still using the mandolin, thinly slice the prepared artichoke into a large bowl. Drain the fennel and add to the artichoke.

Gently mix in the baby spinach, rocket or dandelion, and the herbs. Add the pickled walnuts, preserved lemon and fennel fronds to the salad. Season with salt and pepper.

For the dressing, whisk the walnut oil, mustard and vinegar together and use to dress the salad. Finely grate the walnuts for garnish and sprinkle over the salad. Add the crisp baguette slices.

SERVES 6–8

500g Rough Puff Pastry (see pages 134–137)
8 globe artichokes
4 sweet white onions, very thinly sliced
2 tbsp unsalted butter
1 garlic clove, very finely chopped
1 fresh or dried bay leaf
300ml double cream
200g soft, fresh, rindless goat's cheese
Olive oil, for cooking
150-g piece of aged goat's cheese

TO GARNISH

Seasonal salad leaves
4 radishes, thinly sliced
30ml aged balsamic vinegar

Artichoke and goat's cheese tart

Preheat the oven to 180°C/350°F/Gas 4. Roll out the rough puff pastry to about 5mm thick and cut out your preferred shape. Line a baking tray with baking parchment, then put the pastry in the middle with another piece of parchment on top, and a heavy baking tray on top of the parchment. Bake in the oven until golden and crisp, about 25 minutes. Leave the oven on.

Meanwhile, prepare the artichokes (see page 10 and Note on page 11), keeping the stalk if the artichokes are young or tender. Set aside in a bowl of acidulated water.

Sweat the onions in the butter in a pan until soft, then add the garlic and bay leaf, then the cream. Cook slowly on a low heat until the onions are very soft and the cream has reduced. Remove the bay leaf, add the soft, fresh goat's cheese and blend the mixture to a smooth purée.

Cut the prepared artichokes lengthways into slices the thickness of a pound coin. Quickly sauté in some olive oil in a hot frying pan, then remove and cool. Spoon the onion and goat's cheese purée over the cooked pastry, then arrange the artichokes on top. Heat through in the oven for 3–4 minutes, then remove from the oven and shave the aged goat's cheese over the top. Garnish with the seasonal leaves and sliced radishes, finished with a drizzle of aged balsamic.

SERVES 4

About 150g butter, softened
7 globe artichokes
Plain flour, for dusting
250ml rapeseed oil, for cooking
2 tbsp cornflour
200g egg whites (about 5 large eggs)
90g soft goat's cheese log, cut into 4 pieces
Fine sea salt

Artichoke soufflé

Take 4 ramekins, roughly 8cm in diameter and 4cm deep, and brush generously with half the softened butter. Place in the fridge until set. Remove from the fridge and brush again with butter, then return to the fridge.

Prepare the artichokes (see page 10 and Note on page 11) and set one aside in a bowl of acidulated water. Place the remaining artichokes in a saucepan and cover with cold water. Add 1 tablespoon sea salt and cook on a medium-high heat until tender when pierced with a small, sharp knife. Drain and cool.

Thinly slice the reserved artichoke lengthways and toss in a little plain flour. Heat the rapeseed oil in a pan and, when hot, add the artichoke slices and cook until golden and crisp. Drain on kitchen paper.

Place the cooked artichokes in a blender and blend until very smooth. Transfer to a saucepan and heat gently. Mix the cornflour with enough water to make a thick paste, then whisk this into the artichoke purée and cook, stirring, until thickened. Transfer to a bowl and cover the mixture with cling film to prevent a skin from forming.

Preheat the oven to 180°C/350°F/Gas 4.

Whisk up the egg whites to stiff peaks with a pinch or two of salt. Add 2 large spoonfuls of the cooled artichoke purée to a mixing bowl and whisk by hand to remove any lumps. Add a large mixing spoonful of the whisked egg white and whisk it through, then gently fold in the remaining whisked whites.

Spoon some of the mixture into the prepared ramekins to half-fill them, then add a piece of goat's cheese to each and top with more soufflé mixture. Smooth off the tops with a palette knife and bake for 8 minutes. Serve with the artichoke crisps crumbled onto the top.

SERVES 4

8 globe artichokes
200ml olive oil, plus extra for cooking
2 banana shallots, cut into small dice
1 carrot, cut into small dice
200g smoked bacon lardons
3 garlic cloves, chopped
2 fresh or dried bay leaves
1 tbsp juniper berries
1 fennel bulb, cut into 8 wedges, or 6 pieces of baby fennel, with fronds reserved
200ml gin
2 tbsp unsalted butter
2 tbsp chopped tarragon
2 tbsp chopped flat-leaf parsley
4 sea bream fillets
Sea salt and freshly ground black pepper

Gin-braised artichokes and sea bream

Prepare the artichokes (see page 10 and Note on page 11) and cut lengthways into slices the thickness of a pound coin. Set aside in a bowl of acidulated water.

Heat the olive oil in a large braising pan and add the shallots, carrot and lardons. Sweat for a few minutes, then add the garlic, bay leaves and juniper berries. Add the artichoke slices and fennel wedges, then turn up the heat and add the gin.

Evaporate the alcohol, turn down the heat, then add some cold water or vegetable stock to come part-way up the vegetables. Season the liquid lightly, put a round of baking parchment over the vegetables (a cartouche) and simmer slowly until the fennel and artichokes are just tender. Strain the vegetables, reserving the cooking liquid, and keep them warm.

Return the cooking liquid to the pan and reduce until the flavour has intensified (be careful that it doesn't reduce too much and become too salty), then whisk in the butter and add the herbs. Meanwhile, pan-fry the sea bream in a little olive oil and season with salt and pepper.

Return the vegetables to the pan and coat in the sauce, then serve immediately with the sea bream.

Chicken

Jointing a chicken, or breaking it down into six to eight pieces, is a skill that is often overlooked, as the pieces are so easy to buy ready-prepared. However, buying a whole chicken and jointing it yourself is simple, quick, and much more cost effective. You are left with the added bonus of chicken wings and the fresh carcass, perfect for the base of a chicken soup or roast chicken gravy.

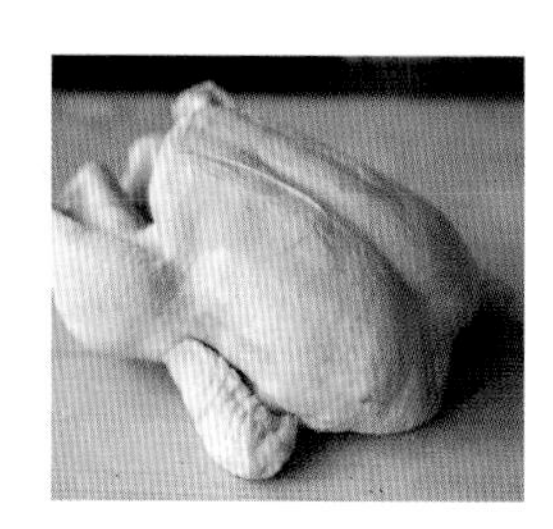

1 Remove any innards and giblets from inside the chicken, and reserve. Pull away the skin at the neck of the chicken. Using a sharp knife, cut a triangle through the flesh to reveal the wishbone and pull it out.

2 Pull the wings away from the breast and cut down through the joints to remove.

3 Pull the legs away from the body and cut down through the joints to remove.

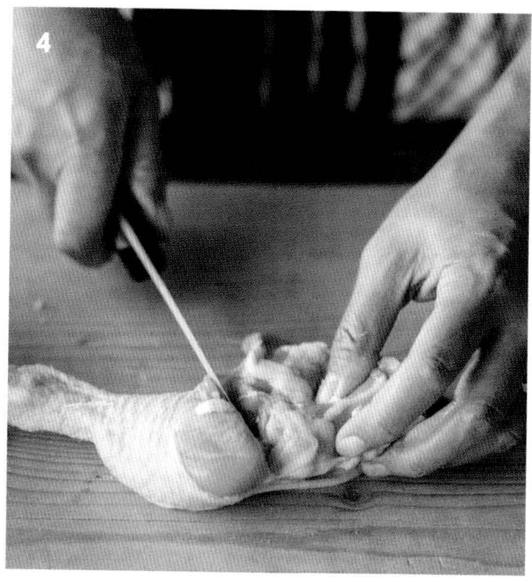

4 Turn the legs over and cut through the thigh joint to separate the pieces into thighs and drumsticks.

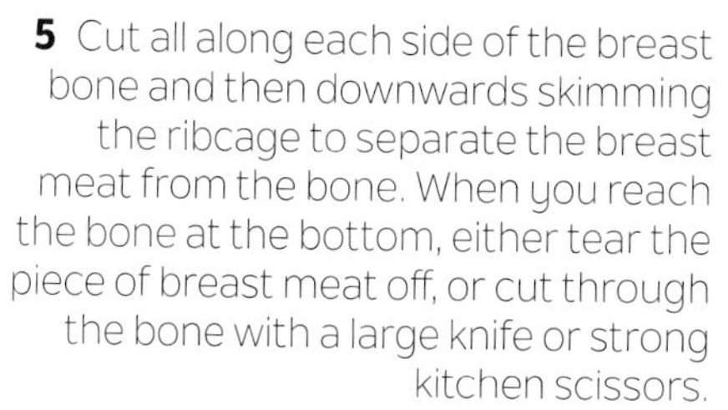

5 Cut all along each side of the breast bone and then downwards skimming the ribcage to separate the breast meat from the bone. When you reach the bone at the bottom, either tear the piece of breast meat off, or cut through the bone with a large knife or strong kitchen scissors.

6 You should now have 8 pieces of chicken.

SERVES 4

450g boneless chicken thighs (see pages 18–19)
30ml dark soy sauce
30ml runny honey
150g brown rice
300ml water
Pinch of salt
½ tsp virgin coconut oil
1 tsp black sesame seeds
1 tsp pumpkin seeds, roughly chopped
2 medium bok choy, or 8 miniature
Sesame and rapeseed oil, for cooking
Coriander leaves, to serve

Soy and honey chicken with brown rice

Put the chicken thighs in a deep saucepan and cover with the soy and honey. Place on a medium heat (it's important to start in a cold pan so the meat stews in the liquid as it cooks. If the pan is hot it will seal the meat and caramelise the honey and soy too quickly and it can get too bitter before the meat is cooked). Heat until the chicken is cooked through.

Meanwhile, put the rice and water in a saucepan with the salt and bring to the boil, then turn down to a gentle simmer, cover and cook until soft and fluffy. Fluff with a fork and stir through the coconut oil and sesame seeds. Sprinkle the chopped pumpkin seeds on top.

When nearly ready to serve, sauté the bok choy in a little sesame and rapeseed oil. Serve the chicken with the rice and bok choy, sprinkled with coriander.

Buttermilk chicken and cornbread

SERVES 4

500ml buttermilk
Juice of 1 lemon
1 tbsp salt
1 medium chicken, about 1.5kg, jointed into 8 pieces (see pages 18–19)
Olive oil, for cooking
200g plain flour
1 tbsp smoked paprika
1 tbsp English mustard powder
Freshly ground black pepper

CORNBREAD

300g plain flour
300g yellow polenta
20g baking powder
12g salt
475ml milk
4 large eggs, lightly beaten
225g unsalted butter, melted, plus extra for greasing
60g maple syrup
100g chopped jalapeño peppers
200g sweetcorn kernels
225g mature Cheddar, grated

TO SERVE

Maple syrup
Finely sliced spring onions
Coriander leaves

Mix the buttermilk, lemon juice and salt together in a bowl. Add the chicken pieces to submerge, cover and chill in the fridge overnight.

The next day, for the cornbread, preheat the oven to 180°C/350°F/Gas 4. Mix the flour, polenta, baking powder and salt together in a large bowl. Mix the milk, eggs, melted butter and maple syrup in a separate bowl. Gradually add the wet ingredients to the dry until fully incorporated. Fold in the peppers, sweetcorn and Cheddar. Grease a medium ovenproof frying pan or skillet with butter and pour in the batter. Bake for 30–40 minutes until lightly golden on top and cooked through in the centre.

To cook the chicken, reduce the oven temperature to 160°C/325°F/Gas 3 and heat the olive oil to 170°C in a deep-fryer or other suitable deep, heavy pan. Mix the flour, smoked paprika and mustard powder together in large bowl, with some pepper. Remove the chicken from the buttermilk and toss well in the flour mixture. Cook in the hot oil until coloured and crispy, then transfer to a wire rack over an oven tray and finish cooking in the oven for 30 minutes.

Serve the chicken with a drizzle of maple syrup, spring onions and coriander, with the cornbread on the side.

SERVES 8

2 litres Chicken Stock (see page 211)
1 medium chicken, about 1.5kg, jointed into 8 pieces (see pages 18–19)
4 red peppers, peeled, quartered and deseeded
4 red chillies, halved, cored and deseeded
3 jalapeño chillies, halved and deseeded
2 tbsp olive oil
2 white onions, finely diced
5 garlic cloves, chopped
2 x 500g tins white hominy corn, or kernels from 2 yellow corn cobs
Juice of 3 limes
Sea salt and freshly ground black pepper

TO GARNISH

Finely sliced iceberg lettuce
Coriander leaves
Crushed tortilla crisps
Lime wedges
Diced avocado
Thinly sliced red radishes

Chicken, corn and lime soup

Heat the Chicken Stock in a pan and season well with salt. Add the chicken pieces and simmer gently until cooked, about 10 minutes for the breast pieces and 40 minutes for the legs, removing the breast pieces when they are cooked. Reserve the cooking liquid.

Ladle some of the cooking liquid into a separate pan and heat. Add the peppers and chillies and cook until soft, then blend the mixture.

Heat the olive oil in a separate saucepan, add the onions and garlic and sweat until cooked. Add the pepper and chilli mixture with all the remaining chicken braising liquid. Shred the chicken meat into the stock and add the corn and lime juice. Adjust the seasoning and serve with the garnishes.

Note: You can thicken this soup with the Coriander and Lime Mayonnaise on page 110, whisking it in at the end before adding the chicken pieces.

Chicken tartiflette

SERVES 4

CHICKEN

2 tbsp olive oil
1 medium chicken, about 1.5kg, jointed into 8 pieces (see pages 18–19)
1 onion, sliced
1 head of garlic, cut in half horizontally
200ml white wine
2 litres Chicken Stock (see page 211)
1 thyme sprig
2 fresh or dried bay leaves
Sea salt and freshly ground black pepper

TARTIFLETTE

1kg waxy potatoes, such as Charlotte, sliced 1cm thick
2 tbsp olive oil
200g smoked Alsace bacon lardons
1 large sweet white onion, thinly sliced
3 garlic cloves, chopped
50g plain flour
300ml double cream
400g curly kale, blanched and roughly chopped
300g Reblochon cheese, broken into pieces, plus 100g extra for the top

Heat a large sauté pan on a high heat, add the olive oil then the chicken pieces, skin-side down, and colour all over for 5 minutes. Remove the chicken from the pan and add the onion and garlic, sweating the onion until softened. Add the white wine and reduce until almost evaporated. Add the Chicken Stock, thyme and bay. Season with salt and pepper and bring the liquid to a very low simmer.

Add the chicken pieces and cook very gently until the breast pieces are just cooked, about 10 minutes. Remove the breast pieces from the pan with some of the broth and leave to cool in the broth. Continue to simmer the leg meat until cooked, about another 30 minutes. Take off the heat and leave to cool in the broth.

Preheat the oven to 200°C/400°F/Gas 6. For the tartiflette, simmer the potato slices in boiling, salted water until almost tender, then drain and set aside.

Heat the olive oil in a pan, add the lardons and cook until coloured, then remove from the pan and add the onion. Cook until translucent, then stir in the garlic. Add the flour and cook for 2 minutes. Add the cream with 200ml of the reserved strained chicken braising liquid and slowly bring to a simmer. Remove from the heat and season with salt and black pepper.

Remove the chicken meat from the bones and cut into large pieces. Fold the chicken through the cream mixture, along with the kale, the 300g cheese and the potatoes. Put into a baking dish, top with the 100g cheese and bake until golden brown.

Game birds

Learning how to butcher game birds is especially useful during the autumn months when they are in abundance. You can apply the same techniques to many birds – pigeon, turkey, duck, pheasant, partridge, even grouse – but it's just a little more fiddly when the birds are little. The possibilities once you know how to do this are numerous, for example leaving them whole and tied, ready to roast; removing the legs and deboning them, ready to stuff and cook.

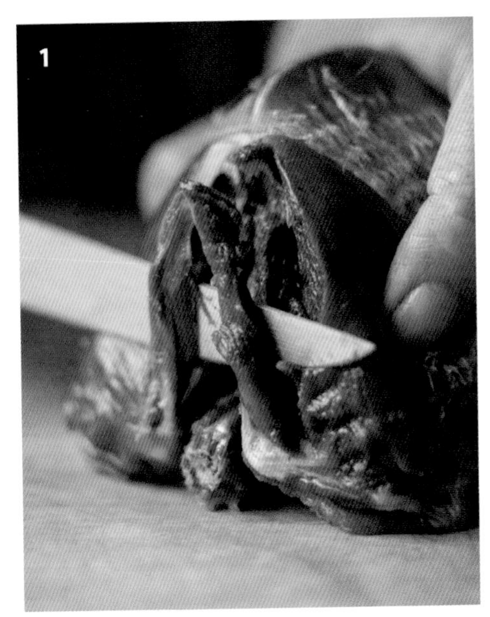

1 If the bird still has its feathers, hold it firmly and pluck the feathers away from you. Remove any innards and giblets from inside. I like to reserve the livers and hearts, either to use in the same recipe or for another. Cut away the skin at the neck of the bird. Feel for the wishbone. Using a sharp knife, cut out the wishbone and pull it away.

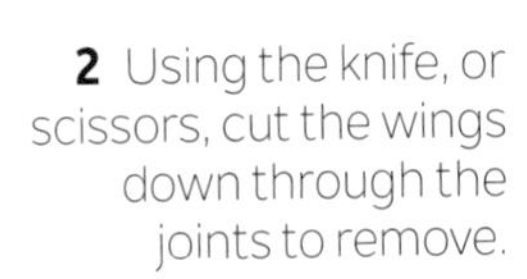

2 Using the knife, or scissors, cut the wings down through the joints to remove.

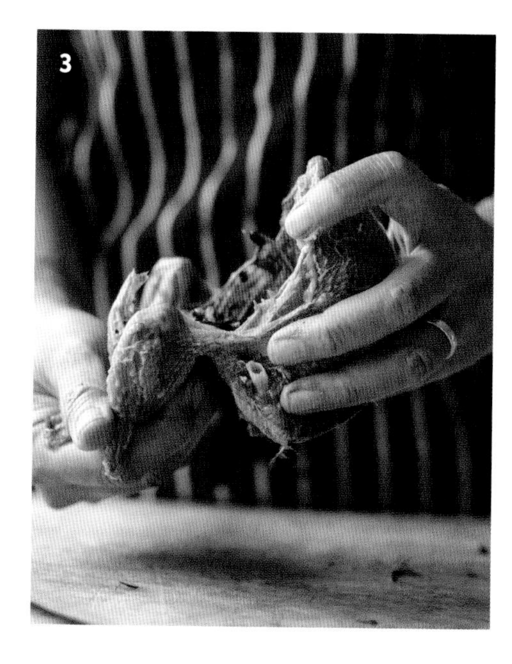

3 Remove the legs by pressing them backwards and then cutting all the way through the hip joint.

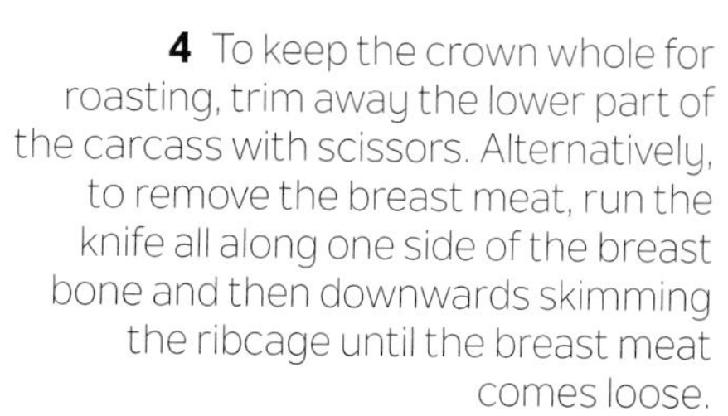

4 To keep the crown whole for roasting, trim away the lower part of the carcass with scissors. Alternatively, to remove the breast meat, run the knife all along one side of the breast bone and then downwards skimming the ribcage until the breast meat comes loose.

5 Use butcher's string to tie the breast to the crown so that the bird keeps its form and the skin doesn't shrink back during cooking.

SERVES 4

4 whole pigeons, plucked and innards removed (see page 26)
1.5 litres water
3 tbsp honey
1 lemon, quartered
3 tbsp dark soy sauce
250ml mirin
100ml rice wine vinegar
250ml vegetable oil

Peking pigeon

Separate the skin of the pigeons from the flesh to loosen but still keeping it attached and trying not to tear any holes in it.

Put the water into a large pot with the honey, lemon, soy sauce, mirin and rice wine vinegar, bring to the boil, then simmer for 20 minutes.

Using a butcher's hook or ladle, lower the pigeons into the pan of simmering liquid for just 3 seconds. Alternatively, place the pigeons on a rack with a tray underneath and baste the pigeons liberally with the basting liquid.

Chill in the freezer for a few minutes to cool rapidly and repeat the basting and cooling process one more time. Transfer to the fridge for 2 hours, or overnight.

Preheat the oven to 200°C/400°F/Gas 6 and place the pigeons in a skillet or roasting tray. Heat the oil to 200°C, taking care. Very carefully ladle the hot oil over the pigeons to crisp up the skin; it will pop and crack. Transfer to the oven for 4 minutes, then leave to rest for 10 minutes before serving whole or cut on the bone into 4 pieces.

SERVES 4

1 whole partridge, plucked and innards removed (see page 26)
2 rashers of thin, streaky bacon
Olive oil, for cooking and dressing
1 tbsp salted butter
3 Brussels sprouts, leaves separated
4 cooked chestnuts, thinly sliced
Sea salt and freshly ground black pepper

CHESTNUT PURÉE

125g cooked chestnuts
1 tsp butter
250ml Chicken Stock (see page 211)

PEARS AND SAUCE

2 small Conference pears
400ml red wine
Zest and juice of 1 orange
80g granulated sugar
1 cinnamon stick
4 cloves
2 cardamom pods
1 star anise
200ml brown chicken stock
Knob of butter

CRUMBLE

1 tbsp crushed pistachios
1 tbsp chopped cooked chestnuts
1 tbsp crushed feuilletine biscuits

Partridge in a pear tree

Remove the legs and wings from the partridge (see pages 26–27), keeping the breast on the bone. Wrap the bacon around a stainless steel baking rod or mould and cook, turning, under a hot grill until crispy; set aside.

For the chestnut purée, put the chestnuts and butter in a pan and cook until coloured, then add the stock and simmer for about 8–10 minutes. Blitz until smooth, adding extra stock if needed. Keep warm.

For the pears and sauce, peel the pears and place in a small pan with the wine, orange zest and juice, sugar, cinnamon, cloves, cardamom and star anise. Bring to the boil, then simmer until cooked through, about 20 minutes. Leave to cool in the liquid, then remove and reserve the pears. Strain 200ml of the cooking liquid into a pan and reduce to a thick consistency. Add the stock and reduce to a good sauce consistency, then remove from the heat and whisk in the butter. Set aside and keep warm.

Preheat the oven to 190°C/375°F/Gas 5. Heat a non-stick ovenproof frying pan and drizzle in a little olive oil. Place the partridge skin-side down in the pan to colour. Turn over and sear on the other side. Add a knob of butter and transfer to the oven for 5–6 minutes, then remove and leave to rest for 5 minutes before removing the breasts from the pigeon.

Pour out the cooking butter from the pan, add a fresh knob of butter and heat until just bubbling. Add the crumble ingredients to the pan and stir into the butter. Spoon over the partridge breasts.

Quickly toss the sprout leaves in a little oil or butter seasoned with salt and pepper.

To serve, cut the pears into pieces your preferred size. Place some chestnut purée on a plate. Place the partridge, bacon and the pears on the purée and sprinkle the sprout leaves over and around. Finish with a drizzle of the sauce, serving the rest on the side.

SERVES 10–12

TERRINE

4 wood pigeon breasts (see pages 26–27)
4 partridge or 2 grouse breasts (see pages 26–27)
200g venison loin
100ml brandy
100ml port
150g chicken or rabbit livers, trimmed
500g minced game meat (passed twice through a mincer on a large setting with 300g lardo)
100g pistachios, blanched
2 tbsp chopped shallots
Olive oil, for cooking
2 tsp thyme leaves
30 rashers of streaky bacon, flattened out a little to lengthen and thin
Sea salt and freshly ground black pepper

Thinly sliced country bread, toasted, to serve

Mixed game terrine

Preheat the oven to 180°C/350°F/Gas 4. Cut the breasts and loin meat into thick strips. Put into a bowl with the brandy and port, season with salt and pepper and set aside. Chop the livers into thick pieces and mix with the minced game meat and pistachios.

Cook the shallots in a little olive oil without colouring them. Add the thyme, then mix through the minced game and liver mixture. Season well.

Use the thinned bacon rashers to line a terrine mould, with enough overhanging the edges to fold over the top, then press the two mixtures into the lined mould, in layers, until full. Cover completely with the overlapping bacon.

Place in a roasting tray half-filled with water (i.e. a bain marie), cover the terrine with foil and bake for about 1 hour 15 minutes, until cooked. Remove the foil for the last 10 minutes.

Leave to cool before turning out. Slice and serve with the toasted bread.

SERVES 4

4 whole jumbo quail, plucked and innards removed (see page 26)
Olive oil, for rubbing
2 knobs of butter
Sea salt and freshly ground black pepper

SALAD

15 fresh hazelnuts in shells, roasted then shelled
400g raw butternut squash, peeled and julienned
1 small red onion, finely sliced
2 tbsp dried cranberries
2 tbsp roughly shredded flat-leaf parsley

BRINE

500ml water
160g sea salt
80g granulated sugar
1 rosemary sprig
2 thyme sprigs
Rind of 1 orange
1 cinnamon stick
2 star anise
2 cloves

DRESSING

1 tbsp wholegrain mustard
2 tbsp white wine vinegar
1 tbsp honey
3 tbsp olive oil
2 tbsp hazelnut oil

Quail with hazelnuts and butternut squash

For the salad, set aside 4 of the roasted hazelnuts and roughly chop the rest. Mix these with the remaining salad ingredients and set aside. Mix the dressing ingredients together and set aside.

Bring the brine ingredients to the boil, then set aside to cool. Spatchcock the quail by cutting up the back with a pair of scissors and flattening it out with your hand. Place in a large bowl, cover with the cooled brine and chill for 20 minutes. Remove, pat dry, rub with a little oil and season with a little salt and pepper. Cook on a hot griddle pan, skin-side down first, for 2–3 minutes on each side.

Meanwhile, finely chop the 4 reserved hazelnuts, put into a small pan with the butter and cook to nutty brown. Mix the dressing ingredients together, add to the salad and mix. Serve the quail drizzled with the hazelnut butter, and the salad alongside.

Steamed pigeon, fennel and tarragon suet pudding

SERVES 6

16 pigeon legs and thighs (see pages 26–27)
100g white onion, sliced
Grated zest of 1 lemon
5 tarragon sprigs, leaves snipped, stalks reserved
1 tbsp extra virgin olive oil
1 medium fennel bulb, thinly sliced, trimmings reserved

SUET PASTRY

Butter, for greasing
300g self-raising flour, plus extra for dusting
1 tsp fine sea salt
140g shredded suet
150ml cold water
1 egg yolk, for brushing

SAUCE

20g unsalted butter
100g white onion, sliced
100ml dry white wine
150ml Chicken Stock (see page 211)
1 star anise
100ml double cream
1 tsp salt
1 tsp ground white pepper
2 tsp lemon juice

TO SERVE

A few tarragon leaves, chopped
A few tomatoes, chopped

Bone the legs of birds by separating the thigh from the leg meat; reserve the bones. Mix the leg and thigh meat with the sliced onion, lemon zest, tarragon and olive oil, cover and refrigerate overnight.

For the suet pastry, generously butter and flour a 1.2-litre pudding basin. Mix the flour, salt and suet together in a bowl, then add the cold water to make a soft dough. Set aside a quarter of the pastry and roll out the remaining dough to a large circle about 1cm thick. Use to line the prepared basin, with a 1-cm border overhanging the rim.

Mix the sliced fennel into the pigeon and marinade and put into the pastry-lined basin. Roll out the remaining pastry until big enough to cover the top. Seal the edges together with a little of the yolk, pressing them together. Cut out a circle of greaseproof paper and place over the pastry, then cover loosely but firmly with foil, leaving room for the pastry to rise but making sure the foil will stay in place. Transfer the pudding to a boiling hot steamer and cook for 2½ hours.

For the sauce, break up the reserved bones and colour in a pan with the butter. Add the reserved fennel trimmings and tarragon stalks with the sliced onion. When nicely coloured, deglaze with the wine and reduce, then add the stock and star anise and cook for about 30 minutes. Strain through a fine sieve, return to the pan, add the cream and cook for a further 15 minutes. Season with the salt and pepper, add the lemon juice and blitz just before serving over the turned-out pudding, with a few chopped tarragon leaves and chopped tomatoes.

Pork belly

We often associate pork belly with bacon, and although it is easy to make your own (see page 40), pork belly has much more to offer. Buy a fresh pork belly on the bone, remove the bones in one piece and cook as pork ribs, or chop them up as the base for a great pork sauce.

1 Lay the pork belly skin-side down. Using a small, sharp knife, start to cut just under the row of ribs.

2 Cut all the way along and begin to pull the ribs away.

6 Flip the pork over, skin-side up. Cut a straight line lengthways down the skin, about one-third of the way across. Do not cut the flesh underneath.

7 Work the knife under the larger portion of skin and start to pull the skin away. Remove the whole portion of skin and discard.

8 Turn the piece of pork back over and trim off any excess fat.

3 Lift the ribs and gently cut underneath them.

4 Cut until you have opened out the piece of pork like a book.

5 Pull away the rack of ribs and reserve.

9 With the skin-covered part of the pork furthest away from you, roll up the meat like a Swiss roll.

10 Turn the roll over, so that the skin-covered part is facing up. Tie some kitchen string around the roll.

11 Tie string at regular intervals along the roll.

SERVES 5–6

1kg pork belly, ribs removed (see pages 36–37, Steps 1–5)
3 thyme sprigs, leaves only
1 rosemary sprig, leaves chopped
Olive oil, for cooking
1 small onion, roughly chopped
1 carrot, roughly chopped
2 celery stalks, roughly chopped
3 litres Chicken Stock (see page 211)
3 fresh or dried bay leaves
3 rosemary sprigs
5 thyme sprigs
1 tsp peppercorns
2 tbsp butter
Sea salt and freshly ground black pepper

BLACK APPLE BUTTER

500g Granny Smith apples, peeled, cored and chopped into small pieces
150ml cider
100g black treacle
50g Demerara sugar
2 tsp mixed spice
Juice of 1 lemon

Rolled pork belly with black apple butter

For the black apple butter, place all the ingredients in a large pan and stew gently until the apples are completely broken down. When most of the liquid has evaporated, transfer to a blender and blitz. Cool and store refrigerated.

Preheat the oven to 140°C/275°F/Gas 1. Remove two-thirds of the pork skin (Steps 6–8 on page 36). Season the inner side of the belly well with 1 tsp salt and some pepper, and sprinkle the thyme and rosemary over the pork. Roll up the belly, skin-side out. Tie tightly at intervals with butcher's string (see Steps 9–11).

Heat a little olive oil in a deep braising pan and add the pork to colour on all sides. Remove from the pan, add the onion, carrot and celery to the pan and colour. Add back the pork with the stock, herbs, 1 tbsp salt and the peppercorns. Bring to a gentle simmer, then transfer to the oven, cover and cook until tender, about 2½–3 hours. Leave to cool in the cooking liquid, then remove the pork to drain on a wire rack and take off the string. Roll tightly in cling film into a firm cylinder and leave to cool in the fridge, ideally overnight. Strain the cooking liquor into a pan and reduce to a thick sauce consistency.

Cut the set pork into slices and gently pan-fry in olive oil until golden, adding some black apple butter to coat all over just at the end of cooking. Heat some of the reduced sauce, add the butter and whisk through.

Serve the pork with the reduced sauce, with a selection of seasonal vegetables of your choice.

MAKES A LARGE QUANTITY

2.25kg pork belly, ribs removed (see pages 36–37, Steps 1–5)
50g flaky salt
12g sodium nitrite
60g maple syrup
50g dark brown sugar

TO SMOKE

60g wood chips
1 tbsp dried rosemary
1 dried bay leaf

Maple smoked bacon

Use a blow torch to burn off any hairs on the pork belly. Use a metal skewer or carving fork to poke holes all over the skin and meat. This allows the marinade to soak in properly.

Mix the salt, sodium nitrite, maple syrup and sugar together and pack onto the pork on both sides. Put into a food bag, seal and place in the fridge for 7 days, turning it every other day.

After 7 days, rinse the pork and dry it, then leave it in the fridge, unwrapped, for 24 hours to dry out.

Transfer the pork from the fridge to a wire rack. Put the wood chips in a roasting tray with the rosemary and bay leaf. Put the wire rack on top and place over a gas hob. When it starts to smoke, cover with aluminium foil, pierce the foil in a couple of places and hot-smoke gently on a very low heat for about 15 minutes. Turn the heat off and seal it completely, then leave to sit for 1 hour. The bacon is now ready to slice and cook.

SERVES 6

About 375g floury potatoes, such as King Edward
20g butter
250g cooked pork belly, shredded
200g leftover cooked vegetables, roughly chopped
Plain flour, for coating
Olive oil, for cooking
Salt

Roasted pork and vegetable hashcakes

Cook the potatoes in boiling, salted water until tender, then drain. Leave to cool a little, add the butter, and mash. Mix in the shredded pork and cooked vegetables and leave to cool. Season with salt.

Shape the mixture into round cakes and lightly coat in flour. Heat some olive oil in a frying pan, add the hashcakes and fry until golden on both sides. Drain on kitchen paper and serve.

SERVES 5

2 oranges
2 cloves
1 star anise
2 cinnamon sticks, crushed
½ tsp freshly grated nutmeg
2 tbsp light brown sugar
50g sea salt
1kg pork belly, ribs removed
(see pages 36–37, Steps 1–5)

Orange spiced pork

Finely grate the zest of 1 of the oranges then peel both oranges. Mix the grated zest with the spices. Roughly chop the orange flesh and add to the spices. Mix in the sugar and salt.

Score the pork skin using a sharp knife and rub the orange spice mixture into the pork on both sides. Place skin-side up in a deep roasting tray and set aside for a couple of hours, or overnight in the fridge.

When you are ready to cook, preheat the oven to 230°C/450°F/Gas 8. Roast the pork skin-side up in the roasting tray for 1 hour, then reduce the oven temperature to 120°C/250°F/Gas ½ and cook for a further 1 hour 15 minutes. Leave to rest for 10 minutes before serving.

SERVES 15

500g pork belly skin (see pages 36–37)
Vegetable oil, for deep-frying

RED PEPPER JAM

100g red peppers, cored, deseeded and roughly chopped
50g red chillies, deseeded and roughly chopped
500g jam sugar (sugar with added pectin; this is important)
300ml cider vinegar

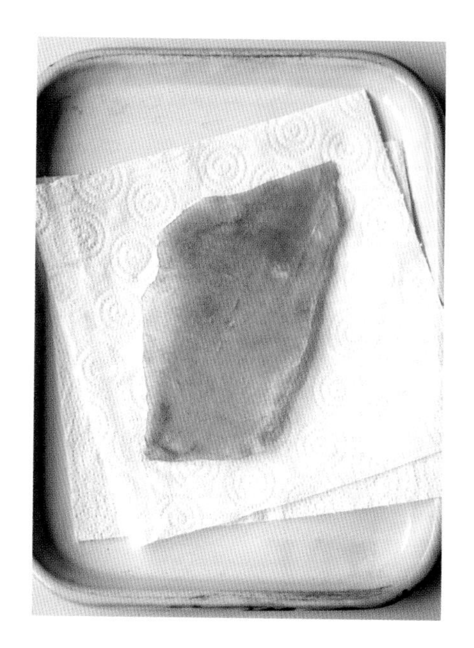

Pork skin scratchings with red pepper jam

For the red pepper jam, put the peppers and chillies in a food processor and blitz until very finely chopped. Dissolve the sugar in the vinegar in a large pan, then stir in the pepper mixture. Bring to the boil and boil for 10 minutes, then remove from the heat and let it cool. Test a small amount of the mixture to be sure it sets. If not, boil for a few minutes more and test again. Put into a sterilised jar.

Place the pork skin in a large pan of water and cook until soft, which can take a while so you may need to top up with hot water. Test with the sharp tip of a small knife and if the skin is soft enough to pierce easily without too much force, it is done. Remove from the heat and leave to cool in the cooking liquor.

When cool, drain, scrape off all the fat and place on trays. Place in a dehydrator on medium-high heat until completely dried, or overnight in a very low oven at 90°C/195°F/Gas ¼.

Break or cut into pieces the desired size. Heat the oil to 180°C in a deep-fryer or other suitable deep, heavy pan. Drop the pieces of pork skin in and cook until they puff up and float to the surface. Drain on kitchen paper and serve with some red pepper jam.

Lamb saddle

Removing the bone from a lamb saddle can seem daunting, but like any butchery, it becomes easier with practice. You also gain the bone at the end of it – great for intensifying your lamb sauce, soup or stock.

1 Place the saddle skin-side down. If the kidneys are still there, pull them out and reserve them in case you need them for your recipe.

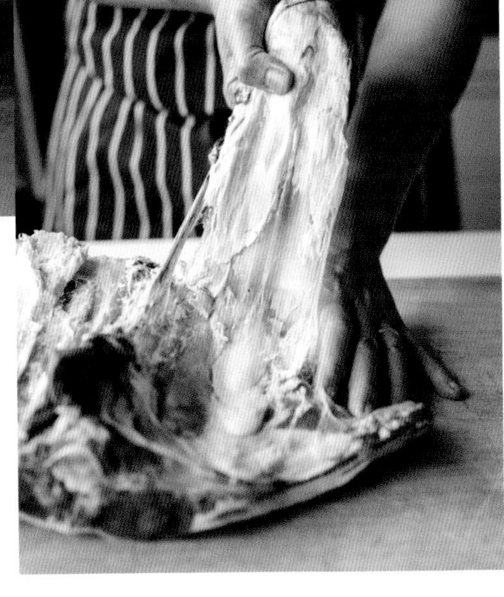

2 Pull away the whole kidneys and excess fat on both sides of the backbone.

3 Take a sharp knife and trim away any sinew, including along the backbone. You want to expose the fillets on either side.

5 Feel for the ribs, under the fillet you've just loosened, with the edge of the knife and cut between the ribs and the fillet all the way along. Do not remove the fillet; just separate it from the bone. Repeat Steps 4 and 5 on the opposite side.

4 Place the tip of the knife at one end of the backbone, on one side of it. Cut gently against the bone and work your way down. Cut only to the depth of the backbone.

6 Work the knife underneath the ribs, all the way along.

7 Cut as close to the ribs as possible so that you're not cutting into the precious loin meat underneath. You want to reach the backbone.

8 Repeat Step 7 on the opposite side of the meat.

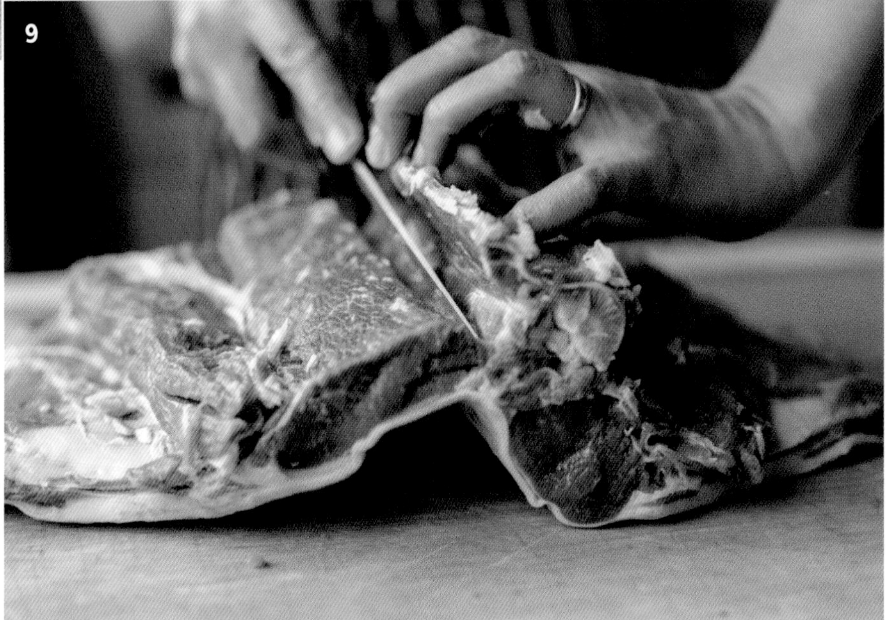

9 You should now be able to see the whole backbone structure. Cut through the last of the flesh still attached to the backbone without cutting all the way through to the skin.

10 Flip the saddle skin-side up. Fold it up like a book and lay the backbone down. Cut along the top of the backbone where it is still attached to the meat.

11 When you have cut all the way down, the bone structure will come away from the saddle.

12 Lay the boneless saddle skin-side down and you can now see the 2 fillets and 2 loins neatly sitting on the skin and ready to be rolled up. The loose sections on each far side are the belly flaps.

13

13 Roll up the saddle.

SERVES 5–6

2–4 lamb's kidneys
2 tbsp rapeseed oil
1 lamb saddle, deboned (see pages 46–49)
300g pork caul or caul fat (order from your butcher)
2–3 tbsp butter
1 rosemary sprig
2–3 garlic cloves, peeled
Sea salt and freshly ground black pepper

GREMOLATA

10g finely grated lemon zest
10g finely grated orange zest
2 tsp thyme leaves
1 garlic clove, very finely chopped
20g Parmesan, grated
20g breadcrumbs
50g chopped flat-leaf parsley
30g chopped mint

Lamb saddle stuffed with gremolata and kidneys

Preheat the oven to 160°C/325°F/Gas 3. Mix the gremolata ingredients together and set aside.

Cut the white sinew from the kidneys, then cut into bite-sized pieces. Heat a frying pan on a high heat, season the kidneys and add some of the oil to the pan. Add the kidneys and sauté quickly, just until coloured, then remove to a colander to drain.

Open the lamb saddle, with the pork caul underneath it, and put the 2 small fillets in the centre, where the bone used to be. Season well with salt and pepper, then smother the meat with the gremolata in an even layer. Arrange the kidneys in a line in the centre, on top of the fillets. Tightly roll the lamb in the pork caul and tie with butcher's string at intervals to hold it together, making sure the stuffing isn't leaking out of the ends.

Season the lamb, heat a large ovenproof frying pan on a medium heat and add the remaining rapeseed oil. Sear the lamb until golden brown all over. Add the butter, rosemary and garlic to the pan, transfer to the oven and roast for 20 minutes, turning the lamb every 5 minutes. Leave to rest for 15 minutes before carving into slices. Serve with vegetables.

Roast saddle and rack of lamb with pressed belly terrine

SERVES 6–8

LAMB BELLY TERRINE

Reserved lamb belly (see below)
1 tbsp dried espelette pepper
1 garlic clove, very finely chopped
Thyme leaves
Plain flour, for coating
Olive oil, for cooking
Sea salt and freshly ground black pepper

LAMB

2 racks of lamb
2 lamb saddles, with belly flaps (see pages 46–49)
2 tbsp rapeseed oil
500g salted butter
2 heads of garlic, cut in half horizontally
2 rosemary sprigs
Sea salt and freshly ground black pepper

LAMB SAUCE

50g unsalted butter, plus a knob for cooking
2 banana shallots, very finely chopped
1 garlic clove, crushed
1 thyme sprig
200ml white wine
500ml lamb stock

For the terrine, preheat the oven to 120°C/250°F/Gas ½. Remove any small bones or extra fat on the belly flaps. Put the meat on a tray and season both sides with the espelette, salt, pepper, garlic and thyme leaves. Line a loaf tin with a piece of baking parchment and layer the meat into it, pressing down between each layer. Put a piece of baking parchment, then foil on top of the meat and place another loaf tin on top, pressing down on the meat. Cook in the very low oven for about 3 hours, until cooked.

Remove from the oven, leave to rest for 30 minutes, then put in the fridge to chill overnight, leaving the weight on top.

The next day, preheat the oven to 170°C/325°F/Gas 3.

Heat a large ovenproof frying pan until hot and season the lamb racks and saddles. Add the oil to the pan and sear the lamb on all sides. Add the butter, garlic and rosemary and, once the butter is foaming, arrange the racks in the same way in your pan, with the saddles the same way up as well. Roast in the oven for 15 minutes, turning every 5 minutes, then remove the racks to rest and continue roasting the saddles for a further 10 minutes, then remove to rest. Discard the roasting butter and keep the roasting pan.

For the sauce, add the knob of butter and the shallots to the roasting pan. Cook on low, scraping the bottom of the pan to remove the roasting bits of meat. Add the garlic and thyme and, once the shallot is cooked, add the wine and turn up the heat to evaporate the alcohol. Reduce to a glaze, then add the lamb stock and reduce by half. Adjust the seasoning, then add the butter to thicken and enrich.

Remove the chilled terrine from the loaf tin and slice a piece. Lightly flour the slice and then pan-fry in some olive oil, colouring until golden brown and being careful not to break the meat apart as you cook. Serve the lamb with the terrine and sauce.

SERVES 2

2 garlic cloves, peeled
2 tbsp harissa paste
1 tbsp honey
50ml olive oil
1 tsp thyme leaves
50g roasted red pepper, chopped
100g rye bread, broken into pieces
1 lamb saddle, sides trimmed
(see pages 46–49)

MINT PESTO

100g mint leaves
20g flat-leaf parsley
20ml lemon juice
½ garlic clove
40g almonds, toasted and crushed
50g Parmesan, grated
100ml olive oil
Sea salt and freshly ground black pepper

Harissa barbecued lamb with mint pesto

Put all the ingredients for the mint pesto in a blender and blitz until smooth. Adjust the seasoning and set aside.

Preheat the oven to 160°C/325°F/Gas 3 and a barbecue on high. Put the garlic, harissa, honey, olive oil, thyme, red pepper and rye bread in a food processor and blitz to a smooth paste. Add a little salt and black pepper and set aside.

Season the lamb saddle and barbecue for 1 minute on each side. Remove to a roasting tray, apply a thick coating of the harissa paste mixture to the top of the lamb and roast in the oven for 12 minutes (depending on the size of the saddle), turning halfway through cooking. Remove and leave to rest for 5 minutes before carving to serve.

Lamb Wellington

SERVES 4

Bunch of large leaf spinach
1 lamb saddle, deboned to give 2 loins (see pages 46–49), bones and trimmings reserved for the lamb jus below
3 tbsp English mustard
Mushroom Duxelles (see page 210)
1 rolled sheet of Rough Puff Pastry (see pages 134–137)
1 egg yolk, lightly beaten, for brushing
Sea salt and freshly ground black pepper

CREPES

240g plain flour
1 tsp salt
4 eggs
250ml milk
250ml water
3 tbsp chopped chives
4 tbsp melted butter
Clarified butter or rapeseed oil, for cooking

LAMB JUS

Bones and trimmings from the lamb saddle, chopped into small pieces
2 tbsp rapeseed oil
2 banana shallots
200g button mushrooms, sliced
1 head of garlic, cut in half horizontally
1 fresh or dried bay leaf
1 rosemary sprig
2 thyme sprigs
1 tbsp tomato purée
200ml white wine
750ml lamb or chicken stock
1 tbsp butter

For the crêpes, sift the flour and salt into a large bowl. In another bowl, whisk together the eggs, milk, water and chives. Whisk the wet ingredients into the flour and stir in the melted butter. Leave to rest in the fridge for 1 hour.

Meanwhile, blanch the spinach in boiling, salted water and refresh in iced water. Dry the spinach and lay out on a piece of cling film, overlapping the leaves until you have a rectangle of spinach measuring 12 x 10cm.

Season the lamb loins with salt and pepper and sear in a very hot pan. Remove and immediately chill.

To cook the crêpes, heat a large non-stick frying pan until very hot, then brush with a little clarified butter or rapeseed oil. Add enough batter to just coat the surface of the pan, colour the bottom side and flip, cooking for a further 15 seconds. Remove the crêpes to a tray lined with baking parchment and reserve.

Continued overleaf...

Brush the chilled lamb all over with the mustard. Wrap each loin individually in the spinach, rolling up the cling film around each one and securing them tightly into a cylinder. Chill in the fridge for an hour or so.

Make a 12 x 10cm rectangle of crêpes, overlapping slightly in the centre. Spread a 1-cm thick layer of Mushroom Duxelles mixture over the crêpes. Remove the cling film from the lamb, place in the centre of the crêpes and roll carefully to completely cover. Trim any excess crêpe from the sides, wrap the lamb tightly in cling film and leave overnight in the fridge.

For the lamb jus, preheat the oven to 160°C/325°F/Gas 3. Roast the bones and trimmings in a roasting tray until nicely golden. Heat a medium saucepan, add the rapeseed oil then the shallots and mushrooms. Cook until coloured, then add the garlic, bay, rosemary and thyme. Add the tomato purée and cook on a low heat for a few minutes. Add the roasted bones and trimmings, then deglaze the pan with the wine, scraping the roasting tray and adding some of the stock. Add the rest of the stock and bring to a simmer. Simmer until reduced by half, then strain into a clean saucepan and reduce until it has reached a sauce consistency. Add the butter, to enrich, and set aside.

Roll out the rough puff pastry to about a 16-cm square. Remove the cling film from the lamb and place in the centre of the pastry. Brush the pastry with the egg yolk and wrap the lamb in the pastry, tucking the pastry in at the sides, trying not to overlap it too much. Brush the Wellington all over with the egg yolk and put in the fridge to rest for at least 2 hours. (This can be done up to a day ahead of time.)

When you are ready to cook, preheat the oven to 220°C/425°F/Gas 7. Score the Wellington with the back of a small knife and cook in the oven for 20–22 minutes. Let it rest for 10 minutes before carving. Serve with the reheated lamb jus.

Round fish

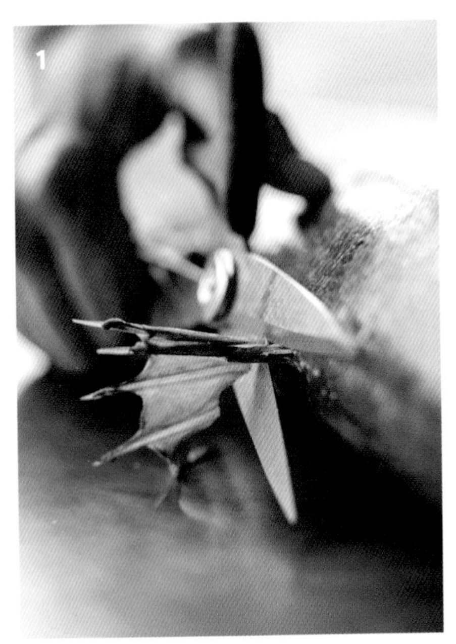

2 Use a fish scaler or the back of a knife to descale the fish: hold the tail and scrape the scales off from tail to head. This will be messy!

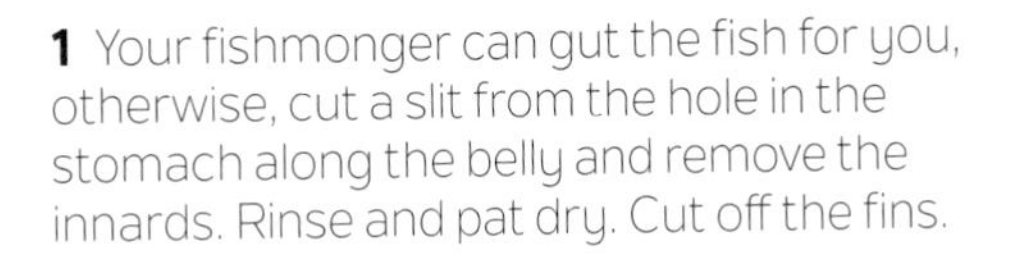

1 Your fishmonger can gut the fish for you, otherwise, cut a slit from the hole in the stomach along the belly and remove the innards. Rinse and pat dry. Cut off the fins.

3 Use a sharp filleting knife to cut through the fish just below the gills until you reach the bone.

4 Make an incision from the top of the backbone all the way to the tail.

Note: When you're buying your whole fish, check that the eyes are clear and gills are a bright red colour; there is no 'fishy' smell, and little smell at all; and the flesh should be firm when you touch it, and not too soft.

5 Open the incision and run the knife against the bones of the fish to start to separate the fillet from the rest of the fish. Keep the knife as close as possible to the bones so as not to waste any of the fillet.

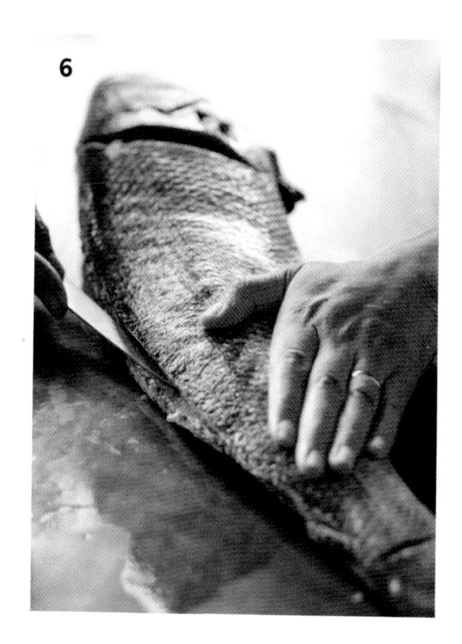

6 Repeat Steps 3–5 on the other side of the fish.

7 You should now have 2 neat fish fillets. Use a pair of fish tweezers to pluck out any pin bones along the length of the fillets. Rinse the fillets and pat them dry before using.

SERVES 6

2 sea bass, 500g each (see pages 58–59)
Olive oil, for brushing
Sea salt and freshly ground black pepper

DRESSING

30ml light soy sauce
1 tbsp honey
Grated zest and juice of 1 blood orange
Grated zest and juice of 1 lime
1 tsp fennel seeds, toasted and ground
50ml extra virgin olive oil

TO FINISH

1 blood orange, peeled, segmented and cut into small pieces
50g fresh pomegranate seeds
Fennel pollen

Sea bass ceviche, orange and pomegranate

Preheat the oven to 160°C/325°F/Gas 3. Remove the skin from the prepared sea bass fillets and set aside. Thinly slice the fillets, cover and set aside in the fridge. Pick the fronds of the fennel bulb and set aside in a bowl of iced water.

Line a baking tray with baking parchment and brush with some olive oil. Season the fish skin with salt and lay on the parchment. Top with another piece of parchment and another baking tray, sandwiching the skin in between. Bake for about 15 minutes, until crispy. Remove to a plate lined with kitchen paper and set aside.

For the dressing, whisk together the soy sauce, honey, orange zest and juice, the lime zest and juice, ground fennel seeds and olive oil. Add salt and pepper to taste.

Break the crispy fish skin into pieces. Gently mix the sea bass slices with the dressing, then spread the fish out on a plate. Sprinkle the fish with the pieces of blood orange, the pomegranate seeds, crispy fish skin and some fennel pollen.

SERVES 2

1 yellow beetroot
1 red beetroot
100ml buttermilk
Mixed salad leaves (such as red endive, frisée or rocket), to serve

SALMON

2 pinches of finely grated lime zest
Pinch of finely grated lemon zest
20g sea salt
10g brown sugar
1 small beetroot, grated
160-g piece of very fresh salmon

MUSTARD DRESSING

½ tsp wholegrain mustard
1½ tsp honey
1 tbsp olive oil
1 tsp white wine vinegar

HORSERADISH CREAM

150ml whipping cream
10g freshly grated horseradish
Sea salt and freshly ground black pepper

Beetroot cured salmon with horseradish

For the salmon, mix the lime and lemon zest, salt, sugar and beetroot together, then use to coat the salmon and place in the fridge for 20 minutes.

Stir the ingredients for the mustard dressing together and set aside.

Place both beetroots in a saucepan with water to cover and a pinch of salt. Cook until tender, about 15 minutes. Peel while still warm, then cut into small wedges.

For the horseradish cream, whip the cream to soft peaks, stir in the grated horseradish and add salt and pepper to taste.

Dress the salad leaves and beetroot with the mustard dressing and arrange on plates. Slice the salmon and add to the plates, then finish with a quenelle of horseradish cream and the buttermilk.

SERVES 4

Bunch of grape vines with leaves
300g coarse salt
1 large cod fillet (about 800g)
(see pages 58–59)
4 tbsp butter
400g smoked bacon lardons
200g baby onions, peeled
400g button mushrooms
4 garlic cloves, crushed
2 fresh or dried bay leaves
1 thyme sprig
250ml red port
500ml red wine
500ml beef stock, reduced to 100ml
2 tbsp chopped flat-leaf parsley
Rapeseed oil, for cooking
Sea salt and freshly ground black pepper

Roast cod in grape leaves

Soak half of the grape leaves in hot water for 10 minutes. Drain and mix with the unsoaked leaves.

Sprinkle the coarse salt all over the cod fillet and leave to cure in the fridge for 30 minutes, then rinse and pat dry. Preheat the oven to 220°C/425°F/Gas 7.

Meanwhile, heat half the butter in a large frying pan and add the lardons and onions. Let them take on some colour, then add the mushrooms and garlic to the pan and sauté until lightly coloured. Add the bay leaves and thyme.

Turn up the heat and add the port and red wine. Reduce the liquid by half, then add the reduced beef stock. Simmer until the onions are cooked through. Season with salt and pepper, then swirl in the remaining butter with the chopped parsley.

Heat a large griddle or grill pan on high and brush the cod fillet with rapeseed oil. Quickly sear the cod fillet on one side and remove to a tray straight away. Spread some grape vines onto a baking tray, nestle the cod in the centre of them and gently cover the fish with more vines. Put the tray into the oven and roast for 10 minutes, until the fish is cooked through.

Remove the fish to a plate, cover with the sauce and serve.

SERVES 4

200g sour cream
1 tbsp chopped chives
2 fresh sweetcorn cobs
110g self-raising flour
1 medium egg, separated
30ml milk
Rapeseed or olive oil, for cooking
A knob of butter (optional)
4 portions of salmon fillet (see pages 58–59)
Sea salt and freshly ground black pepper
Hollandaise (see page 108), to serve

Salmon with sweetcorn fritters

Mix the sour cream and chives together with some seasoning and keep chilled.

Slice off the kernels from the sweetcorn cobs and place in a bowl with the flour. Mix in the egg yolk and milk. Whisk the egg white to stiff peaks and fold into the corn mixture.

Heat a little oil, with the butter if you like, in a frying pan until hot. Dollop spoonfuls of the fritter mixture into the hot pan and pan-fry on a medium-low heat until golden brown on both sides. Keep warm.

Heat a non-stick frying pan on a medium-high heat and add a little oil. Season the salmon with a little salt and pepper and pan-fry, skin-side down, for 2 minutes. Turn and cook for another minute (if you like your salmon more well cooked, then add a couple more minutes).

Serve the salmon with the sweetcorn fritters and Hollandaise.

SERVES 4

1 whole brown trout, gutted and scaled
(see page 58, Steps 1–2)

ASPARAGUS SALSA

1 bunch of English asparagus
3 heirloom tomatoes (red, yellow, green), peeled, deseeded and cut into 1-cm dice
½ red onion, cut into 1-cm dice
½ cucumber, peeled, deseeded and cut into 1-cm dice
½ mild red chilli, deseeded and cut into small, thin strips
1 lime
2 tbsp white balsamic vinegar
Tabasco sauce, to taste
2 tbsp chopped coriander leaves and some stems

PESTO

1 small bunch of flat-leaf parsley
½ bunch of mint
1 garlic clove
100g pine nuts, toasted
80g Parmesan, grated
150ml extra virgin olive oil
Grated zest of ½ lemon and 20ml juice
Sea salt and freshly ground black pepper

Grilled whole trout, asparagus salsa and pesto

For the pesto, put all the ingredients into a blender and blend until smooth. Add seasoning to taste and set aside.

For the salsa, snap off the asparagus spears at the tip and set aside. Slice the remaining stems into small, thin rounds about 2mm thick. Put into a bowl with the tomatoes, red onion, cucumber and chilli.

Remove the skin and pith from the lime and cut out 3 of the segments. Shred the segments into fine pieces and add to the asparagus mixture. Add the balsamic and a few drops of the Tabasco, to taste. Season with a pinch of salt and a few turns of the pepper mill. Thinly slice the reserved asparagus tips.

Preheat a non-stick griddle or grill pan. Remove the gills, eyes and fins from the trout, lightly oil the skin, then place on the hot griddle or grill pan and cook for 4–5 minutes on each side, until just cooked.

Place the salsa in a small bowl and serve with fresh coriander and the sliced asparagus tips tossed in the juices of the salsa.

Lobsters

The UK benefits from a source of native lobsters, perfect for a special occasion. Easier to prepare than whole crabs, lobsters provide large pieces of delicious meat with less work. The heads and shells can be used in sauces and stocks, or to make a lobster-flavoured butter or vinaigrette for a salad.

To cook your lobster, see page 70.

2 Twist the tail until it comes away from the head and set aside.

1 Twist the claws of your cooked lobster until they come away from the head and set aside.

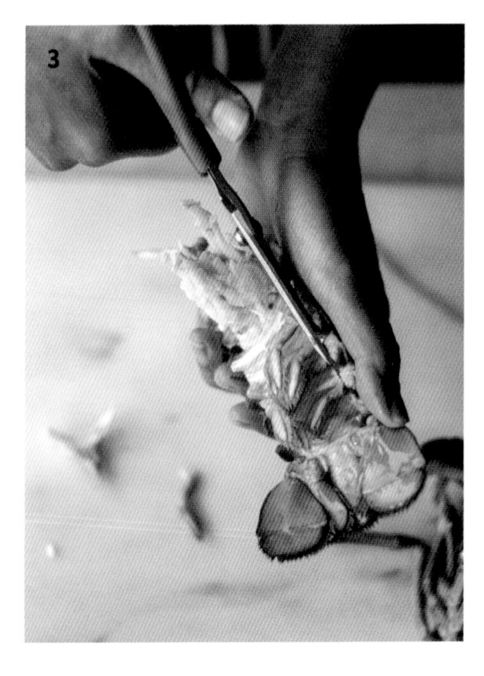

3 Turn the tail piece over and use kitchen scissors to cut along either side of the tail shell.

4 Pull the softer belly shell away to expose the meat inside. Pull the meat out in one piece.

5 Snap the pincers apart.

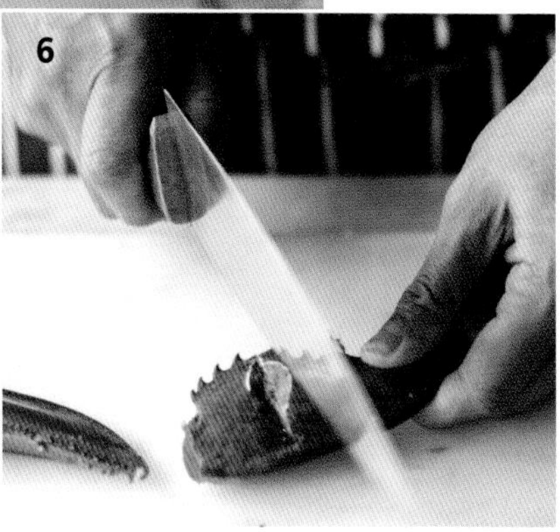

6 Crack the remaining part of the claw using the back of a large knife or lobster crackers.

7 Remove the meat from the claws in one piece.

8 Remove the difficult pieces of meat from the claws with a lobster pick.

9 Reserve both the meat and the lobster shells for your recipe.

Crabs

Extracting the meat from a whole crab is a time-consuming job – picking all the meat out of the legs, claws and body, double-checking for bits of shells, etc. But the flavour makes it worth it, and you get the additional bonus of the crab shells to make a flavourful bisque or stock as a base for other dishes. Remember to use all the juice that is extracted from the body, as it imparts loads of flavour.

Cooking crabs and lobsters

Always choose a crab or lobster that feels heavy for its size and smells fresh. They are best cooked immediately after killing, so ask your fishmonger to kill them for you, then cook them as soon as you can. Never buy a dead, uncooked crab or lobster, as you don't know when it was killed and it may no longer be safe to eat.

Bring a large pan of well-salted water to the boil. Add the crab or lobster and simmer for 11 minutes per kg for crab or 8 minutes per 600g for lobster. Leave the crab (but not the lobster) to cool a little in the liquid. Transfer to a tray, place in the fridge and leave to cool.

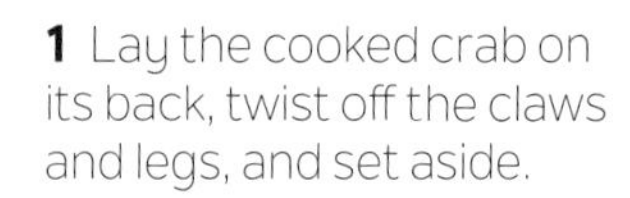

1 Lay the cooked crab on its back, twist off the claws and legs, and set aside.

2 Use the palm of your hand to push down on the crab. Pull the broken shell and insides away – it will come off in one piece. Pull away the dead man's fingers (i.e. the feathery gills) found inside the shell and around the body.

3 Scoop out the brown meat into a bowl.

4 Use a large knife to cut the main body in half.

5 Use a lobster pick or skewer to pick the white meat out of the cavities and put in a separate bowl.

6 Crack the claws and legs using the back of a large knife or a kitchen mallet.

7 Remove the meat from the claws. Finish by picking through the crab to check for any stray shells.

Lobster rolls

SERVES 6–8

BUN DOUGH

20g butter
200ml milk
100ml water
500g plain flour
12g dried yeast
12g salt
35g caster sugar
1 egg yolk

GLAZE

1 egg, beaten
1 tbsp milk

FILLING

3 tbsp mayonnaise
1 tbsp ketchup
1 tbsp brandy
1 tbsp finely chopped shallots
1 tbsp chopped tarragon
1 tbsp chopped chives
1 tbsp wholegrain mustard
Lemon juice
300g cooked lobster meat (see pages 68–69)
Sea salt and freshly ground black pepper

1 little gem lettuce, finely sliced, to serve
1 Granny Smith apple, finely sliced, to serve

For the bun dough, melt the butter in a pan with the milk and water. Put the dry ingredients (including the yeast) in a stand mixer bowl with a hook attachment. Add the egg yolk, then the milk mixture and mix on a low speed. Once combined, mix on medium speed for 8 minutes until smooth. Cover the bowl and leave to prove for 1 hour, or until doubled in size.

Preheat the oven to 200°C/400°F/Gas 6.

Remove the dough to the work surface and knead for 1 minute. Cut the dough into 100-g pieces, roll each piece into a ball, then roll each ball into a log shape and put on an oiled baking sheet about 1cm apart. Mix the egg and milk together for the glaze and use to brush each bun. Bake for about 20–25 minutes, until golden brown, then leave to cool on a wire rack.

Meanwhile, for the filling, mix the mayonnaise, ketchup, brandy, shallots, herbs and mustard together, with lemon juice and salt and pepper to taste. Put the lobster meat in another bowl and add as much of the mayonnaise mixture as you need to bind the lobster. Cut the buns from the top, almost all the way through, and fill with the lobster mixture. Top with the lettuce and apple to serve.

SERVES 4

2 lobsters, 500g each, uncooked
Lobster Stock (see page 210)
Rapeseed oil, for cooking
100g smoked bacon lardons
2 garlic cloves, crushed
1 slice of sourdough bread
3 little gem lettuces, smaller leaves left whole, larger ones cut down
Pickled red onion, to serve
Parmesan shavings, to serve

BISQUE DRESSING

400ml Lobster Bisque (see page 210)
150g egg yolks (about 8 eggs)
100g Dijon mustard
1 garlic clove, chopped
5 anchovy fillets
200g Parmesan, grated
1 tbsp chopped tarragon
Juice of 1 lemon
400g olive oil
400g vegetable oil
Salt

Lobster Caesar salad

For the bisque dressing, put the lobster bisque in a saucepan and reduce to 100ml, then cool. Put the egg yolks, mustard, garlic, anchovies, Parmesan, tarragon, cooled lobster bisque reduction and some lemon juice in a large bowl. Whisk for a few minutes until light and doubled in volume, then slowly start to add the olive and vegetable oils (mixed together in a jug), whisking constantly until it reaches a thick mayonnaise consistency. Season with salt and lemon juice and set aside.

Lightly poach the whole lobsters in the Lobster Stock for 10 minutes (see cooking instructions on page 70) and cool over ice. Once cool, extract the lobster meat (see pages 68–69) and set aside.

Heat 1 tablespoon rapeseed oil in a frying pan, add the lardons, colour, then remove to kitchen paper. Wipe out the pan and add 50ml rapeseed oil with the garlic and, when hot, add the piece of sourdough and colour until crispy. Drain on kitchen paper and cut into croûtons.

Put some bisque dressing on each plate and add some lardons, sourdough croûtons, little gem, pickled red onion, Parmesan shavings and lobster meat and serve immediately.

MAKES 20

100g salted butter, for cooking

DOUGH

1 tsp salt
350g plain flour
1 large egg
3 tbsp sour cream or crème fraîche
200ml lukewarm water

FOR THE FILLING

500g floury potatoes, diced and cooked in boiling, salted water
60g softened butter
50g black truffle, chopped
2 tbsp chopped chives
400g cooked lobster meat (see pages 68–69), finely chopped
1 tbsp crème fraîche
Salt and freshly ground black pepper

Lobster pierogi

For the dough, mix the salt into the flour and make a well in the centre. Add the egg and sour cream to the well, then slowly pour in the water. Using your hands or a fork, bring into a dough and knead until just smooth. Cover the dough and leave to rest in the fridge for at least 30 minutes.

For the filling, mix together all the ingredients. Season to taste.

Roll out the dough until quite thin (about 3mm) then, using a round cutter about 10cm in diameter, stamp out 20 rounds. Add some lobster filling mixture to the centre of each round and pinch the sides together to seal.

Cook the pierogi in boiling, salted water until they float to the surface. Remove with a slotted spoon and leave to dry for a few seconds before putting them on an oiled tray. Melt the 100g butter in a frying pan until foaming, and gently fry the pierogi on all sides.

SERVES 6

1 small sourdough loaf, thickly sliced
1 garlic clove, halved
Olive oil, for drizzling
300g freshly picked cooked white crab meat and 80g brown (see pages 70–71)
Micro cucumber flowers, to garnish

CUCUMBER GAZPACHO

4 cucumbers
200ml olive oil
1 green pepper, roughly chopped
3 plum tomatoes, roughly chopped
1 celery stalk, roughly chopped
2 tbsp sherry vinegar
1 tsp celery salt
1 tbsp Worcestershire sauce
6 slices of white bread, roughly torn
100ml tomato juice
200ml Vegetable Stock (see page 211)
Bunch of basil stalks
Sea salt and freshly ground black pepper

Crab with cucumber gazpacho

For the cucumber gazpacho, peel the cucumbers, reserving the skin. Blitz the skin with the olive oil, then strain and keep chilled. Deseed and chop the cucumbers.

Blitz together the chopped cucumbers, pepper, tomatoes, celery, sherry vinegar, celery salt, Worcestershire sauce, bread, tomato juice, stock and basil stalks, with salt and pepper to taste. Pass through a fine sieve and chill in the fridge.

Rub the sourdough slices with the halved garlic clove and drizzle with olive oil. Grill or bake in an oven preheated to 180°C/350°F/Gas 4 until very dry, then cool.

To serve, spread a little brown crab meat onto each toasted bread slice and place in a deep bowl. Add white crab meat on top and pour the chilled gazpacho around the crab croûton. Finish with a drizzle of the cucumber oil, and a cucumber flower.

SERVES 4

1 purple kohlrabi
2 Granny Smith apples
1 lemon, quartered
3 tbsp olive oil
1 sage leaf, finely chopped
150g Mayonnaise (see page 106)
2 tbsp crème fraîche
2 tbsp wholegrain mustard
200g freshly picked cooked white crab meat and 50g brown (see pages 70–71)
1 tbsp aged sherry vinegar
1 tbsp finely chopped chives
Sea salt and freshly ground black pepper

TO GARNISH

Micro coriander
Smoked paprika

Crab, apple and mustard

Slice the kohlrabi and apples into very thin strips, or use a spiraliser. Place in a bowl and add a squeeze of lemon juice, 1 tablespoon of the olive oil, and some salt and pepper.

Whisk the chopped sage into the Mayonnaise, crème fraîche and mustard, and add a squeeze of lemon juice.

Mix the brown crab meat with the sherry vinegar and the remaining 2 tablespoons olive oil to make a split dressing. Mix the chives through the white crab meat and add a squeeze of lemon juice and some salt and pepper.

Place some of the sage mayonnaise mixture on each plate. Add some of the apple and kohlrabi to form a nest. Sit some white crab meat on the nest and finish with some micro coriander. Drizzle over some brown crab dressing and dust with a little smoked paprika just before serving.

SERVES 1

200-g piece of watermelon
200-g piece of cantaloupe melon
Olive oil, for cooking
A knob of butter
100g freshly picked cooked white crab meat (see pages 70–71)
1 tsp chopped red chilli
1 tbsp chopped chives
Tabasco sauce, to taste
1 lime, halved
1 very ripe avocado
1 small fennel bulb, with fronds reserved
1 small wholemeal loaf, thinly sliced
1 preserved lemon, cut into small dice
Sea salt and freshly ground black pepper

Crab and melon salad

Preheat the oven to 180°C/350°F/Gas 4. Pan-fry both melon pieces with a little olive oil and the butter, then set aside to cool and cut into cubes.

Mix the crab meat with the chilli, chives, and Tabasco and lime juice to taste.

Blitz the avocado with a few drops of Tabasco, lime juice and some salt and pepper, until smooth. Thinly slice the fennel and place in a bowl of ice cubes with a little water added. Toast the bread slices in the oven until crisp.

To serve, drain and dry the fennel slices and serve the crab with avocado purée and some preserved lemon, the melon cubes, fennel and toast. Lightly season and drizzle with a little olive oil.

Scallops

Buying scallops in their shells is the best way to ensure their freshness. Our local fishmonger will get them fresh from the market if I call up and preorder, so ask yours if they will do the same.

1 Slide a table knife between the scallop shells and slide it gently round to nip the muscle inside. This will pop the scallop open.

2 Push the flatter shell up and remove it.

3

3 Remove the tough, slightly translucent muscle on the side of the scallop by cutting straight down and through it, or loosen it by running your finger around the scallop.

4 Slide the knife under the scallop, then using your thumb to hold down the roe and skirt, lift out the scallop with your other hand. The roe is edible and has a very strong flavour.

5 Pull the scallop out. If it smells bad or is a pale grey, it's not fresh and shouldn't be used.

6 Clean the scallop shells and reserve for serving.

SERVES 4

1 tbsp vegetable or corn oil, for cooking
10g popping corn
Finely grated zest and juice of 1 lime
Pinch of ground cumin
1 pink grapefruit
40g caster sugar
100ml water
1 rhubarb stick
½ small red onion
Finely grated zest and juice of 1 lemon
1 medium fennel bulb, with fronds reserved, finely sliced
8 medium scallops, shelled (see pages 80–81)
1 red chilli, deseeded and finely chopped
2 tbsp olive oil, plus extra to serve
Fennel pollen, to serve
Sea salt and freshly ground black pepper

Scallop ceviche with fennel, rhubarb and pink grapefruit

Heat the oil in a saucepan, add the popping corn, cover with the lid and cook until popped. Remove from the heat and add a pinch each of lime zest and salt, and the cumin.

Remove the pith and skin from the grapefruit, then cut out the segments. Squeeze out the juice from the remains of the grapefruit, place in a small pan and reduce to a thick glaze. Set aside to cool.

Boil the sugar and water together in a pan and set aside to cool. Dice a little of the rhubarb for the garnish and set aside. Thinly slice the rest into ribbons, using a swivel peeler, and place in the cold sugar syrup.

Slice the onion as finely as possible, season with a little salt and lemon juice and set aside. Add the fennel slices to the onion.

Rinse the scallops gently in lightly salted cold water and dry. Cut each one into 6 slices and mix gently through the fennel and onion. Cut the grapefruit segments into small chunks and add to the scallops. Add a pinch or two of chilli, a touch more lime and lemon juice and the olive oil. Season with salt and pepper, mix well and taste – you want to taste the chilli and citrus juices but not be overpowered by them.

Place on a plate, sprinkle with some fennel fronds and a touch of fennel pollen, and the remaining lime zest and the lemon zest. Drizzle some of the grapefruit juice glaze and a little olive oil over, garnish with the drained, diced rhubarb and serve immediately, with the popcorn and ribboned rhubarb.

SERVES 4

150g pumpkin seeds
350ml Vegetable Stock (see page 211)
100ml double cream
3 cooking chorizos, cut into chunks
Rapeseed oil, for cooking
8 medium scallops, shelled (see pages 80–81)
A knob of butter
100g salted almonds, chopped
Fine sea salt and freshly ground black pepper

Scallops with salted almonds and pumpkin seed purée

Place the pumpkin seeds and stock in a saucepan and bring to the boil. Turn down to a gentle simmer and cook until soft, then transfer to a blender and blitz until smooth. Bring the cream to the boil, then add to the blender to blitz for a couple of minutes. Taste and add salt and pepper as needed.

Heat a frying pan, add the chorizo chunks and cook until lightly coloured. Remove, leave to cool, then finely chop, reserving the cooking oil.

Heat a non-stick pan with a drop of rapeseed oil on a medium heat. Rinse the scallops gently in lightly salted cold water and dry. Season them with a little fine sea salt and place in the pan, turning each after 30–40 seconds. Add the butter to the pan, then add the chopped almonds and chorizo.

Place a dollop of the pumpkin seed purée on each plate, followed by 2 scallops, then spoon the almond mixture over the scallops. Drizzle some of the reserved chorizo oil around the scallops to serve.

SERVES 2

300g cauliflower, chopped into small pieces
Rapeseed oil, for cooking
60g butter, plus a knob for the scallops
240ml double cream
2 slices of Parma ham
4 large scallops, shelled (see pages 80–81)
2 tsp chopped shallot
1 tsp grated garlic
2 tsp fine capers
2 tbsp chopped flat-leaf parsley
Sea salt and freshly ground black pepper
Thick crème fraîche, to serve

Scallops with cauliflower and capers

Preheat the oven to 180°C/350°F/Gas 4.

In a pan, cook the cauliflower in a little oil and the butter until soft. Add the cream and bring to the boil, then season with salt and pepper and blitz until smooth in a blender. Keep warm.

Cook the Parma ham on a baking tray in the oven until crisp, about 6–8 minutes. Remove and set aside.

Heat a non-stick frying pan and add a little oil. Rinse the scallops gently in lightly salted cold water and dry. Season the scallops, place in the pan and cook for 30–40 seconds on each side until lovely and golden. Remove the scallops from the pan. Add a knob of butter to the pan with the shallot and garlic and cook for 1 minute. Add the capers and parsley and take off the heat.

Spoon the scallops onto a bed of cauliflower purée, drizzle with the caper butter and add the crisp Parma ham. Serve with a spoonful of thick crème fraîche.

SERVES 5

10 medium scallops, shelled (see pages 80–81)
Rapeseed oil, for cooking
1 tbsp unsalted butter
1 tsp black curry powder (or very mild curry powder mixed with squid ink)

BASMATI PURÉE

80g basmati rice
80g white miso paste
350ml water
½ red chilli, halved lengthways
2cm fresh ginger
1 tsp coriander seeds
Sea salt

RICE PUFFS

400ml vegetable oil
80g wild rice

FRESH LIME AND KUMQUAT SYRUP

3 limes, segmented (peel reserved)
5 kumquats
100g caster sugar
100ml water

Curried scallops with kumquats

For the basmati purée, rinse the rice in cold water until clear. Cook the miso paste in a stockpot on a low heat for 5 minutes, then add the rice and water. Put the chilli, ginger and coriander seeds in a piece of muslin cloth and tie to make a sealed bag. Add to the pan with a little salt, stir the rice well and cook, uncovered, until completely soft. Remove the muslin parcel, strain the liquid from the rice and reserve. Transfer the rice to a blender and add back as much liquid as needed to blend until smooth.

For the rice puffs, heat the vegetable oil in a deep saucepan to 200°C and fry the raw rice until crispy. Remove from the oil with a small sieve and drain on kitchen paper. Season immediately with a pinch of salt.

Continued on page 88...

For the fresh lime and kumquat syrup, blanch the lime peel in boiling water. Blanch and refresh the kumquats 3 times, then quarter and deseed them. Bring the sugar and water to the boil in a saucepan, then add the lime peel, lower to a simmer and cook for 5 minutes. Remove from the heat, add the kumquats and set aside to infuse until you are ready to serve.

Reheat some of the basmati purée, whisking all the time and adding a little water if needed; keep warm. Meanwhile, dress a few lime segments in some of the lime syrup and reserve.

Rinse the scallops gently in lightly salted cold water and dry. Sear the scallops briefly in a little rapeseed oil a large, hot frying pan, then add the butter and curry powder to the pan. Mix well and baste the scallops until cooked and totally black.

To serve, put 2 curried black scallops on each plate with the basmati purée, rice puffs, kumquats and lime syrup.

SERVES 4

Olive oil, for cooking
1 small fennel, roughly chopped
Zest of 2 oranges
Zest and juice of 1 lime
300ml Fish Stock (see page 211)
100g butter, plus an extra knob for cooking
A handful of trompette mushrooms, washed and blanched
A handful of girolle mushrooms, cleaned
8 medium scallops, shelled and sliced in half (see pages 80–81)
100g samphire
100g sea aster
1 punnet of edible seaweed
Salt and freshly ground black pepper

Poached scallops with wild mushrooms

Heat a little olive oil in a saucepan, add the fennel and cook for 2 minutes. Add the orange and lime zest and Fish Stock. Bring to the boil and then simmer gently on a low heat for 5 minutes. Strain through a fine sieve, reserving the cooking liquor.

Place a few tablespoons of the cooking liquor into a small saucepan and heat gently. Whisk in the butter until emulsified.

Sauté the mushrooms in a separate pan with a little olive oil and the knob of butter. Season with salt and pepper.

Rinse the scallops gently in lightly salted cold water and dry. Add them to the emulsified stock and gently poach until tender, 2–3 minutes. Transfer the mushrooms and scallops to serving bowls.

Turn the heat up under the poaching liquor and drop in the samphire, sea aster and seaweed. Cook for 1 minute, then remove from the liquor and place around the scallops. Add a few drops of lime juice to the poaching liquor and spoon onto the scallops.

Squid and cuttlefish

The principles for preparing squid and cuttlefish are the same, and they're much easier than people assume.

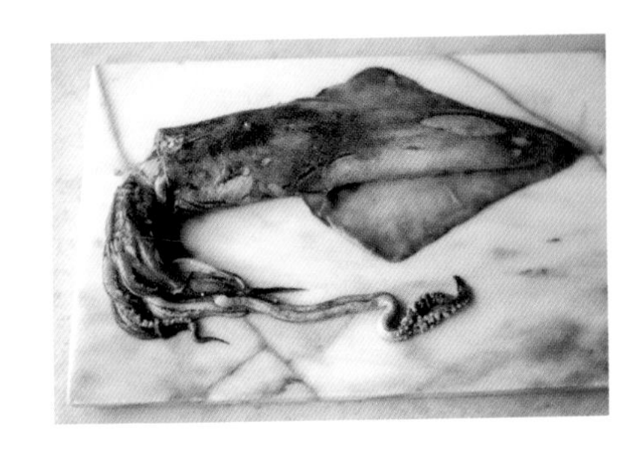

1 Hold the squid up by the body so that the tentacles hang down.

2 Pull the head and tentacles away from the body.

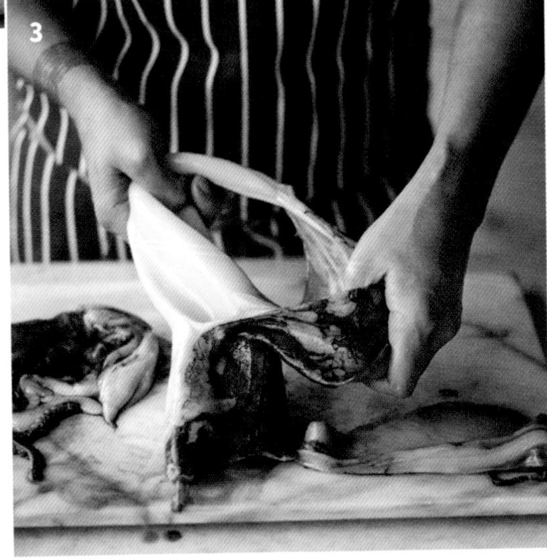

3 Peel the skin off the body.

4 Cut the tentacles off above the eyes and rinse well under cold running water.

5 Pull the innards out, reserving the fragile ink sac if needed.

6 Pull the long thin quill out of the body.

7 Rinse the tentacles and tube well and dry with kitchen paper.

SERVES 6

4 large cuttlefish (see pages 90–91)
Large bunch of flat-leaf parsley, leaves picked
2 tarragon sprigs, leaves picked
200ml double cream
80g Israeli (pearl) couscous
15g cuttlefish ink
Olive oil, for cooking
Sea salt and freshly ground black pepper

Cuttlefish 'tagliatelle' with pearl couscous and herbs

Slice the cuttlefish down one side of each body to open them out flat. Stack one on top of the other, wrap in cling film and freeze. Slice the frozen cuttlefish as thinly as possible.

Blanch the parsley and tarragon leaves in boiling, salted water. Transfer the hot leaves to a blender and blitz until smooth.

Bring the cream to the boil in a pan, then add to the tarragon and parsley and season with salt and pepper.

Cook the couscous in salted water as you would pasta, then drain and stir in the cuttlefish ink.

Heat a non-stick frying pan or griddle on a high heat. Drizzle the sliced cuttlefish with a little olive oil and sprinkle with salt and pepper. Add to the pan or griddle and cook very quickly, for 40–50 seconds.

Place some couscous in each serving bowl and top with the cuttlefish. Pour the parsley sauce around and serve.

Raisin and caper-stuffed squid

SERVES 5

10 small squid tubes (see pages 90–91)

STUFFING

1½ tbsp olive oil
2 salted anchovies, chopped
1 garlic cloves, chopped
½ small white onion, finely diced
½ red chilli, finely chopped
1 fresh or dried bay leaf
75ml white wine
50g capers
50g raisins, chopped
100g sourdough bread, cut into small dice
1 small egg, beaten
2 tbsp chopped flat-leaf parsley
Finely grated zest and juice of 1 lemon

BRAISING LIQUID

2 tbsp olive oil
½ onion, diced
2 garlic cloves, crushed
1 fresh or dried bay leaf
½ tbsp tomato purée
2 tsp caster sugar
100ml white wine
250g tomatoes, peeled, deseeded and diced
125ml water
Sea salt and freshly ground black pepper

TO SERVE (OPTIONAL)

Torn basil leaves
Chopped olives

Heat the olive oil for the stuffing in a large frying pan, add the anchovies and garlic and cook on a low heat for a few minutes. Add the onion, chilli and bay leaf and continue to cook until the onion is translucent. Add the wine and cook to evaporate. Add the capers and raisins and cook for a few minutes. Remove from the heat, take out the bay leaf, and mix the caper and raisin mixture with the bread, egg, parsley, and lemon zest and juice. The mixture should just come together – not too wet and not too dry.

Heat the olive oil for the braising liquid in a large pan and add the onion. Cook until translucent, then add the garlic and bay leaf. Add the tomato purée and sugar and cook for a few more minutes. Add the wine and reduce, then add the diced tomatoes and water and bring to a simmer. Season.

Fill the squid tubes with the stuffing mixture and close the end of each with a cocktail stick. Add all the stuffed squid tubes to the braising liquid and simmer for 1 hour, until tender. Spoon out the squid, remove the bay leaf and blend the braising liquid using a hand-held blender. Serve the sauce with the squid, with some torn basil and chopped olives, if you like.

SERVES 2

5 large black olives, pitted and quartered
5 large green olives, pitted and quartered
2 cuttlefish (see pages 90–91)
2 tbsp broad beans
120g cooking chorizo
4 cherry tomatoes, quartered
2 good-quality piquillo peppers, cut into strips
Olive oil, for cooking
Leaves of 2 marjoram sprigs
Smoked paprika
Sea salt and freshly ground black pepper

Cuttlefish with piquillo and marjoram

Preheat the oven to 180°C/350°F/Gas 4. Keeping the 2 colours of olives separate, place on a tray and cook in the oven for 10 minutes. Leave to cool, then finely chop, still keeping them separate.

Cut down one side of the cuttlefish body, open it out flat and score into the flesh, but not all the way through, then cut into 4 or 5 pieces.

Cook the broad beans in boiling, salted water 3–4 minutes, then leave to cool and slip out of their skins. Place the chorizo in a pan of water, bring to a gentle simmer for 2 minutes, then drain, peel and cut into small dice. Sauté the chorizo dice in a hot frying pan, mix in the broad beans and take off the heat. Add the tomatoes and piquillo peppers and gently mix together.

Sauté the cuttlefish pieces and tentacles in a hot frying or griddle pan with a little olive oil. Season with salt and pepper and serve with the broad bean mixture and olives. Finish with the marjoram leaves and a light dusting of smoked paprika.

MAKES 40, 20G EACH

Olive oil, for cooking
1 small onion, chopped
1 small carrot, chopped
2 large cuttlefish (see pages 90–91), cut into 4
100ml white wine
400ml Fish or Vegetable Stock (see page 211)
3 lemon thyme sprigs
Sea salt

BÉCHAMEL

100g salted butter
100g plain flour
800ml milk (or cuttlefish cooking liquor)
6 egg yolks
30g cuttlefish ink
Sea salt and freshly ground black pepper

TO FRY THE CROQUETTES

50g plain flour
2 eggs, beaten
50g panko breadcrumbs
400ml vegetable oil

Cuttlefish croquettes

Heat a little olive oil in a pan and add the onion, carrot and cuttlefish to colour. Add the wine and bring to the boil, then add the stock. Add the thyme with a pinch of sea salt, cover with a piece of greaseproof paper (a cartouche) and reduce the heat to a gentle simmer. Cook until the cuttlefish is tender, about 1 hour. Leave to cool in the liquid, then remove the cuttlefish, reserving the cooking liquor, and very finely chop.

For the béchamel, melt the butter, stir in the flour and make a thick béchamel with the milk or cooking liquor, Whisk in the egg yolks and bring back to the boil, still whisking. Take off the heat and whisk in the cuttlefish ink. Fold in the chopped cuttlefish, season, then leave to cool.

Pipe the cold mixture onto trays, then cut into large bite-sized portions. Place the trays in the freezer to set.

Coat the set croquettes first in the flour, then the egg, then breadcrumbs, then keep in the fridge. Heat the vegetable oil in a deep-fryer or other suitable deep, heavy pan to 170°C and deep-fry the croquettes in batches, until golden, about 2–3 minutes, turning them halfway through cooking. Serve hot.

SERVES 6

1.5 litres vegetable oil, for deep-frying
12 medium squid tubes (see pages 90–91), cut into thin rings
Sea salt
Roasted Garlic and Saffron Mayonnaise (see page 109), to serve

TEMPURA BATTER

75g plain flour
75g cornflour
1 egg, beaten
60g black curry powder
150ml ice-cold sparkling water

Crispy black squid tempura

For the tempura batter, put both flours in a large bowl. Mix the egg and curry powder together in a separate, small bowl, then add to the flour, along with the sparkling water. Whisk until just incorporated, then leave the batter to rest in the fridge for 20 minutes.

Meanwhile, put the vegetable oil in a deep-fryer or other suitable, heavy pan and heat to 180°C. Dry the squid rings, then dip into the tempura batter. Shake off any excess and fry in the hot oil for a few minutes, turning them over until the batter is crispy. Remove to kitchen paper and sprinkle with salt.

Serve with the Roasted Garlic and Saffron Mayonnaise.

Risotto

A great risotto is the perfect dinner – creamy rice that carries almost any flavour and keeps the integrity of each grain. The difference between a great risotto and an average one is big, however. If it's overcooked it will be mushy and have no texture. If not enough butter and cheese are added at the end, it will be missing that creamy, rich quality.

1 Heat 2 tablespoons olive oil and sweat 1 small, finely chopped onion for 5 minutes, until translucent.

2 Add 300g carnaroli rice. Cook on a low heat until it starts to dry out.

3 Turn up the heat, add 150ml dry white wine and 1 bay leaf and evaporate the wine for 2–3 minutes.

5 After 16 minutes, cook out any liquid and turn off the heat.

4 Begin to add 2 litres hot (light and seasoned) Chicken Stock (see page 211), one ladle at a time, for about 16 minutes, stirring every few minutes, until the rice has just a slight bite.

6 Quickly beat in 1 tablespoon mascarpone and 50g cubed, unsalted butter using a wooden spoon.

7 Stir in 100g grated Parmesan, season to taste and serve immediately. Serves 4.

SERVES 4

1kg fresh clams, rinsed in running water for 2–3 minutes to remove any sand, and drained
200ml dry white wine
2 tbsp olive oil
1 small onion, finely chopped
1 garlic clove, finely chopped
2 spicy cooking chorizos, finely diced
1 fresh or dried bay leaf
300g carnaroli rice
1.5 litres Chicken Stock (see page 211)
50g Parmesan, grated
50g butter
2 tbsp chopped basil
2 tbsp chopped flat-leaf parsley
Salt

Clam and chorizo risotto

Heat a large casserole dish on a high heat and add the clams to the hot dish. Add half the wine quickly, cover with a lid and cook for 2 minutes, until the clams open. Drain and set aside, reserving the cooking liquor.

Heat the olive oil in a medium saucepan, add the onion and garlic and sweat for 5 minutes, until translucent. Add the chorizo and bay leaf and cook for a few minutes. Add the rice and toast for 2 minutes, then add the remaining wine and turn up the heat to evaporate the liquid.

Add the reserved clam cooking liquor, then the Chicken Stock a ladleful at a time, stirring occasionally, until the rice is almost cooked, about 15 minutes.

Evaporate the remaining liquid, then remove from the heat and beat in the Parmesan, butter and fresh herbs. Add the clams just to heat through. Taste and add salt if needed, then serve immediately.

SERVES 4

500g white new potatoes
200g Jerusalem artichokes
2 tbsp olive oil
1 banana shallot, finely chopped
1 garlic clove, finely chopped
30g potato flour
125ml dry white wine
50g unsalted butter
80g Parmesan, grated
2 tbsp mascarpone
2 tbsp chopped chives
2 slices of dry-cured ham
(prosciutto or Serrano)

POTATO AND ARTICHOKE BROTH

Reserved potato and artichoke skins
Vegetable oil, for coating
1 garlic clove, crushed
1 rosemary sprig
Sea salt

Potato and artichoke, 'risotto style'

Preheat the oven to 160°C/325°F/Gas 3. Wash the potatoes and artichokes well, peel, reserving the skins, and finely dice. Place the potatoes in a bowl of cold water and the artichokes in a bowl of acidulated water, and set aside.

Dry the washed potato and artichoke skins well. Coat them in a little vegetable oil, then spread out in a single layer in a roasting tin, with a little salt. Roast in the oven until nicely golden brown all over. Transfer the roasted skins to a saucepan with the garlic and rosemary. Add cold water just to cover, slowly bring to a simmer and cook for 30 minutes. Strain, season with salt, measure out 2 litres and keep hot.

Heat the olive oil for the risotto in a medium saucepan, add the shallot and garlic and sweat until translucent. Drain and add the potato and artichoke dice and cook for 2 minutes without letting them colour, then sprinkle the potato flour over them.

Turn up the heat and add the wine. Evaporate the wine, then start to add some of the potato and artichoke broth, a ladleful at a time, stirring as it cooks. Once the potatoes and artichokes are almost tender, evaporate any remaining liquid. Once tender but still holding their shape, remove the pan from the heat and beat in the butter, Parmesan, mascarpone and chives using a wooden spoon, until you have an emulsified and creamy mixture. Season with salt, if needed.

Meanwhile, place the ham slices under a hot grill until crisp, then drain on kitchen paper and crush into crumbs.

Sprinkle the ham crumbs over the top of the risotto and serve immediately.

SERVES 4

2 tbsp olive oil
1 small onion, finely chopped
300g pearl barley
150ml dry white wine
2 litres Mushroom Broth (see page 212), hot
250g Mushroom Duxelles (see page 210)
100g Parmesan, finely grated
25g mascarpone
50g unsalted butter
2 tbsp chopped chives
2 tbsp cep (porcini) mushroom powder

Pearl barley and mushroom risotto

Heat the olive oil in a medium saucepan, add the onion and sweat until translucent. Add the pearl barley and toast for a few minutes. Turn up the heat, add the wine and evaporate it, then start to add the Mushroom Stock a ladleful at a time, stirring every few minutes, until the pearl barley is almost tender.

Add the Mushroom Duxelles and cook for a few minutes, evaporating any remaining stock. Remove from the heat and beat in the Parmesan, mascarpone, butter and chives using a wooden spoon. Dust with the cep mushroom powder and serve immediately.

Mayonnaise

You can vary the flavour of homemade mayonnaise by changing the oils and vinegars you use to make it. Key points to remember: make sure your ingredients are all at room temperature before you begin – mayonnaise doesn't like extreme changes in temperature, even once it is made; allow time for the egg yolks to increase in volume before you add the other ingredients; and add your oil slowly at first to stabilise the emulsifying process. For hollandaise, see page 108.

1 Whisk 1 medium egg yolk, 1 teaspoon Dijon mustard and 1 tsp white wine vinegar together in a bowl.

2 Mix 150ml rapeseed oil and 30ml olive oil together in a jug. Slowly pour the oils in a thin stream into the bowl, whisking constantly.

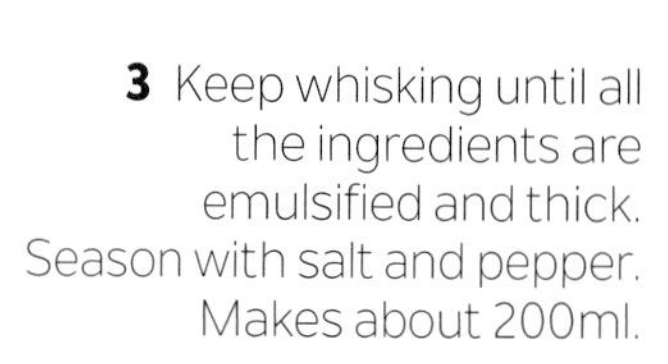

3 Keep whisking until all the ingredients are emulsified and thick. Season with salt and pepper. Makes about 200ml.

Hollandaise

Probably the most famous of all sauces, hollandaise is delicious as it is, but it is also the perfect base for many other delicious sauces. Learning the steps to making perfect hollandaise is important, as it can be tricky to master. Making sure your egg yolks are whisked well over a gentle heat before the fat is added is crucial, as is the amount of fat you are adding – too much and it can split; too little and it tastes solely of egg yolk.

MAKES ABOUT 250ML

100ml white wine vinegar
50ml water
1 tbsp white peppercorns, crushed
3 medium egg yolks
200ml warm clarified butter
½ lemon
Sea salt

Put the vinegar, water and crushed peppercorns into a small pan and reduce by two-thirds on a medium heat, about 3 minutes. Set aside to cool, then strain into a heatproof bowl and whisk in the egg yolks.

Place the bowl over a pan of lightly simmering water and whisk for 5–8 minutes, until very thick and pale. Take off the heat and whisk in the warm clarified butter. Add a squeeze of lemon juice, season with a little salt and serve immediately.

MAKES ABOUT 500ML

300ml rapeseed oil, plus extra for the garlic
100ml olive oil
2 heads of garlic
4 egg yolks
1 tbsp Dijon mustard
1 tbsp white wine vinegar
Pinch of saffron strands
1 tbsp lemon juice (optional)
Sea salt and freshly ground black pepper

Roasted garlic and saffron mayonnaise

Preheat the oven to 180°C/350°F/Gas 4 and mix the oils together in a jug.

Slice the tops off the heads of garlic and sprinkle each one with some salt and a little rapeseed oil. Put the tops back on and wrap each one tightly in foil. Roast in the oven for about 25–30 minutes, until cooked through and sweet. Squeeze the garlic flesh from the skins into a mixing bowl.

Add the egg yolks, mustard and vinegar to the garlic and whisk really well for a few minutes. Start to add the oil gradually, whisking the whole time, until you have a thick mayonnaise (see page 106).

Add 2 tablespoons hot water from the kettle to the saffron and leave to infuse for 2 minutes. Whisk the saffron and its water into the mayonnaise, season well and add the lemon juice if needed.

Photographed on page 111.

MAKES ABOUT 300G

50g creamy blue cheese
150g Mayonnaise (see page 106), made with walnut oil instead of olive oil
100ml double cream, whipped

Blue cheese and walnut dip

Whisk the blue cheese into the Mayonnaise, then fold in the whipped cream.

MAKES ABOUT 500ML

2 bunches of coriander
400ml rapeseed oil
5 egg yolks
1 tbsp Dijon mustard
30ml lime juice
Sea salt and freshly ground black pepper

Coriander and lime mayonnaise

Roughly chop the coriander, put into a blender with the oil and blend for a few minutes. Strain the oil through a single layer of muslin cloth; it may take an hour or so for the oil to slowly trickle through.

Put the egg yolks, mustard and lime juice in a mixing bowl and beat for a few minutes. Start to add the oil gradually and continue until you have a thick mayonnaise (see page 106). Add some water or more lime juice to thin it out if needed. Taste and season.

SERVES 2

MAYONNAISE

2 egg yolks
1 tsp Dijon mustard
1 tbsp white wine vinegar
½ garlic clove, very finely chopped
200ml rapeseed oil
Lemon juice, to taste
Sea salt and freshly ground black pepper

MINESTRONE

2 tbsp olive oil
2 tbsp butter
1 onion, finely diced
1 carrot, finely diced
1 celery stalk, finely diced
3 garlic cloves, finely chopped
½ fennel bulb, finely diced
100g swede, finely diced
100g parsnip, core removed, finely diced
1 thyme sprig
1 rosemary sprig
2 fresh or dried bay leaves
150g cooked haricot beans
Handful of chopped, cooked cavolo nero or spinach
2 tbsp chopped flat-leaf parsley
50g Parmesan, grated

Winter minestrone finished with mayonnaise

For the mayonnaise, whisk the egg yolks, mustard, vinegar and garlic together for 2 minutes. Whisk in the oil, slowly at first, until fully emulsified (see page 106). Season with lemon juice, salt and pepper and adjust the consistency with a little water if it seems too thick (you want a thinner mayonnaise than usual here).

Heat the olive oil and butter in a large saucepan and add the onion, carrot and celery. Sweat for a few minutes, then add the garlic, fennel, swede and parsnip. Sweat for 5 minutes, until just tender. Season with salt and pepper and add the thyme, rosemary and bay leaves. Add enough water to just cover the vegetables and bring to a simmer. Cook until the vegetables are tender, about 40 minutes, then add the beans and the cavolo nero or spinach. Cook for another 5 minutes, then add the parsley. Take off the heat, adjust the seasoning and whisk in the mayonnaise, slowly pouring it into the soup to thicken it slightly. Serve topped with the Parmesan.

SERVES 4

4 blood oranges
Hollandaise (see page 108), warm
2 bunches of asparagus, trimmed
Olive oil, for cooking
Sea salt and freshly ground black pepper

Blood orange maltaise and grilled asparagus

Finely grate the zest of one of the blood oranges into a small saucepan. Squeeze the juice of the remaining 3 oranges into the pan, place over the heat and reduce by two-thirds. Set aside to cool.

Peel the remaining blood orange, remove the skin and cut out the segments with a sharp vegetable knife. Set aside.

Stir the cooled blood orange reduction into the warm Hollandaise.

Line the asparagus spears up in groups of 5 and push a wooden skewer through each group of 5 to secure. Heat a griddle or grill to very hot. Drizzle the asparagus with olive oil and season with salt and pepper. Place on the griddle or grill and cook for 4–5 minutes, turning halfway through. Serve the asparagus hot with the warm maltaise and the orange segments.

Pasta

Making fresh pasta is simple, inexpensive and delicious. A few key points to remember: use a high-gluten flour – '00' or strong white bread flour, for example – to produce the best results and an 'al dente' pasta. The dough can incorporate different liquids to change the flavour, richness and colour of the final product. For example, reduced red wine mixed with egg yolks produces a rich dough which would work well for a meaty ragout. On the other hand, a bright basil purée as the base of a pasta dough would match a summery, fresh tomato sauce topped with melting burrata cheese...

1 Tip 500g '00' pasta flour on the work surface and make a well in the middle.

2 Mix together 3 whole large eggs and 6 large egg yolks, then pour into the flour well.

3 Start to mix the eggs into the flour with a fork.

Note
You can either use the pasta machine to create tagliatelle etc. with your fresh pasta dough, or cut it by hand. Cook the pasta straight away or shape and freeze it, or keep it hanging in a dry area at room temperature where it will keep for 3 or 4 days.

4 Stir in circles, incorporating a little flour at a time.

5 Keep taking more flour into the egg with the fork until everything is incorporated.

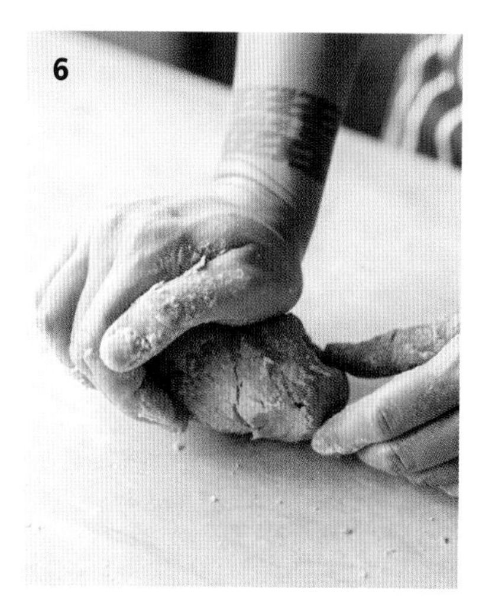

6 Bring together into a dough with your hands. This makes enough pasta to serve 4.

7 Wrap the dough in cling film and leave to rest for 30 minutes. Shape the dough into a small rectangle, flat enough to put through a pasta machine on its thickest setting. Pass the dough through twice on this setting, adding a light dusting of flour in between. Continue to bring the thickness down on the machine and pass the pasta until you have passed it through the thinnest setting.

Onion and sage agnolotti with glazed chicken

SERVES 8

Pasta dough (see pages 114–115)
1 egg yolk and 1 tbsp water, beaten
Polenta, for dusting

CHICKEN AND JUS

2 tbsp rapeseed oil
6 chicken thighs, skin on
2 shallots, sliced
1 Braeburn apple, roughly chopped
½ head of garlic
1 thyme sprig
1 fresh or dried bay leaf
250ml cider
200ml apple juice
400ml Chicken Stock (see page 211)
A knob of butter

ONION AND SAGE FILLING

50g salted butter
4 sweet white onions, finely chopped
1 thyme sprig
1 tbsp water
200ml single cream
300ml whole milk
300g plain white bread, crusts removed and cut into small cubes
A pinch of grated nutmeg
Sea salt and freshly ground black pepper

TO FINISH

1 Braeburn apple, cut into small dice
5 sage leaves
Selection of wild mushrooms, cleaned and trimmed
A knob of butter

Preheat the oven to 140°C/275°F/Gas 1. For the chicken and jus, heat half the rapeseed oil in a large, deep skillet and colour the chicken thighs for 5 minutes. Remove and add the shallots and apple with the garlic, thyme and bay leaf and cook until the shallots are coloured. Add the chicken thighs back to the pan, deglaze with the cider and reduce, then add the apple juice and chicken stock. Cover the contents of the skillet with a round of baking parchment (a cartouche) and bring to a simmer. Transfer the pan to the oven and cook for 1½ hours. Remove from the oven and let the meat sit in the braising liquid for 30 minutes, then remove the thighs and carefully take the bones out. Chill the chicken and braising liquid separately in the fridge overnight.

For the onion and sage filling, melt the butter in a large saucepan and add the onions and thyme. Season with salt and pepper, add the water, cover and cook on a low heat for 20 minutes, stirring occasionally, until soft and sweet. Add the cream and milk and bring to a simmer. Add the bread and nutmeg and cook until you have a thick paste. Remove the thyme and transfer the paste to a blender. Blend until smooth, then transfer to a bowl to cool. Once cold, blitz again (it should be quite thick) and then put into a piping bag.

Heat the remaining rapeseed oil in a frying pan and add the chilled chicken thighs, skin-side down. Cook on a medium heat to crisp the skin, then remove from the pan and cut into small pieces. Strain the braising liquid into a pan and reduce to a sauce consistency. Add the butter and set aside.

Roll out the pasta on the thinnest setting of the machine. Pipe a long line of filling across the bottom of the dough, 2.5cm in from the edge. Brush the pasta with the beaten egg above the line of filling and fold it over, pressing tightly against the filling to remove any air trapped inside. Using your finger, press along the line at intervals to divide into parcels. Cut the pasta along the top of the egg washed area, then through each finger divide to create individual parcels. Transfer each one to a tray dusted with polenta, ready to cook.

Cook the agnolotti for 2 minutes in a large pan of boiling, salted water. Meanwhile, add the crispy chicken to the sauce and reheat gently. Add the apple and sage off the heat. Sauté the wild mushrooms in the butter and season. Gently add the drained agnolotti, coat in the sauce and serve with the wild mushrooms.

SERVES 4–6

3 tbsp olive oil
2 onions, cut into small dice
2 celery stalks, cut into small dice
1 carrot, cut into small dice
3 garlic cloves, chopped
2 fresh or dried bay leaves
1 thyme sprig
1kg lamb shoulder, cut into small dice
1 tbsp tomato purée
125ml white wine
500ml lamb stock
Pasta dough (see pages 114–115), cut into pappardelle
Sea salt and freshly ground black pepper
Chopped flat-leaf parsley, to serve
Grated Parmesan, to serve

Lamb ragoût with fresh pasta

Heat the olive oil in a large casserole dish, add the onions, celery and carrot and sweat until translucent. Add the garlic, bay leaves and thyme. Add the lamb meat, season well with salt and pepper, sweat, then add the tomato purée.

Cook for a few minutes, then deglaze with the wine. Add the lamb stock and simmer for 3 hours, covered, until reduced, adding, more stock or water if it gets too dry as it cooks.

Cook the pasta in boiling, salted water until al dente. Drain and add to the ragoût with parsley and Parmesan.

SERVES 4

Pasta dough (see pages 114–115)
Polenta, for dusting
1 head of broccoli, cut into small florets
100ml olive oil
3 garlic cloves, chopped
1 red chilli, finely chopped
4 salted anchovies, rinsed and chopped
300g cooked chickpeas
20 cod cheeks
1 tbsp chopped flat-leaf parsley
Sea salt
2 tbsp panko breadcrumbs, fried in garlic-infused olive oil, to serve

Orecchiette, chickpeas and cod cheeks

Cut the pasta dough into 4 pieces and roll each piece into a long cylinder about 1cm in diameter. Using a sharp knife, cut each cylinder into 1cm pieces. Use the flat side of a table knife to flatten a piece of dough, then drag the knife slightly towards you over the work surface to form a disc. Repeat with the remaining pieces to form discs, transferring them to a tray dusted with polenta as you work.

Cook the pasta in boiling, salted water until al dente, then drain and set aside, reserving about 200ml of the cooking water. Blanch the broccoli and set aside.

Gently heat the olive oil in a pan and quickly mix in the garlic, chilli and anchovies. Add the chickpeas and broccoli florets to the pan, then add the cod cheeks and cook for another minute or two. Add the pasta to the pan and stir in with the reserved cooking water. Mix in the parsley and serve topped with the fried panko breadcrumbs.

Chestnut tortellini in mushroom and Marmite broth

SERVES 6 AS A STARTER

Pasta dough (see pages 114–115)
Polenta, for dusting
Mushroom and Marmite Broth
(see page 212)
A little extra virgin olive oil
2 handfuls of fresh seasonal mushrooms and a handful of wild garlic, sautéed, to garnish

CHESTNUT PASTA

150g chestnut flour mixed with a pinch of salt
150g '00' pasta flour
10 large egg yolks

CHESTNUT AND MASCARPONE FILLING

1 banana shallot, finely chopped
1 tbsp olive oil
1 tbsp finely chopped rosemary
200g tinned sweet chestnuts, chopped
200g mascarpone cheese, plus extra to garnish
2 tbsp chopped chives
Sea salt and freshly ground black pepper

Make the chestnut pasta using the ingredients above, and following the instructions on pages 114–115.

To make the chestnut and mascarpone filling, sweat the banana shallot in the olive oil until translucent. Add the rosemary and cook for a few more minutes, then add the chestnuts. Season the mixture well and leave to cool. Once cold, fold in the mascarpone and chives and set aside.

Roll out the pasta on the thinnest setting of the machine and cut out about 60 circles, about 8cm in diameter. Put a teaspoon of the filling in the centre and fold up the bottom half of the pasta to make a semi-circle. Pinch the two sides together underneath the filling to make something that resembles a little hat. Transfer the shaped tortellini to a tray dusted with polenta.

Reheat the Mushroom and Marmite Broth if chilled. Meanwhile, cook the pasta in boiling, salted water for 2 minutes, then drain and toss in a bit of olive oil. Put the tortellini in a bowl, garnish with some sautéed seasonal mushrooms and wild garlic and serve with the hot mushroom and Marmite broth. Garnish with drops of mascarpone.

Simple breads

The steps here are for focaccia, but the basics are very similar for most simple yeasted breads. Once you've understood how to work with yeast, how important it is to knead the dough thoroughly enough to activate the gluten in the flour, making for an elastic dough, and how long to leave for proving, which is when fermentation takes place and air bubbles form in the dough, then you can make all sorts of breads and doughs, like bagels, pizza and steamed buns.

1 You will need:
250ml warm water
12g active dried yeast
1 tsp caster sugar
10g salt
500g strong white bread flour,
  in a large mixing bowl
80ml olive oil, plus extra for greasing
30g wild garlic

2 Mix a little of the warm water with the yeast and sugar and leave for about 5 minutes for the yeast to activate – it will start to bubble gently.

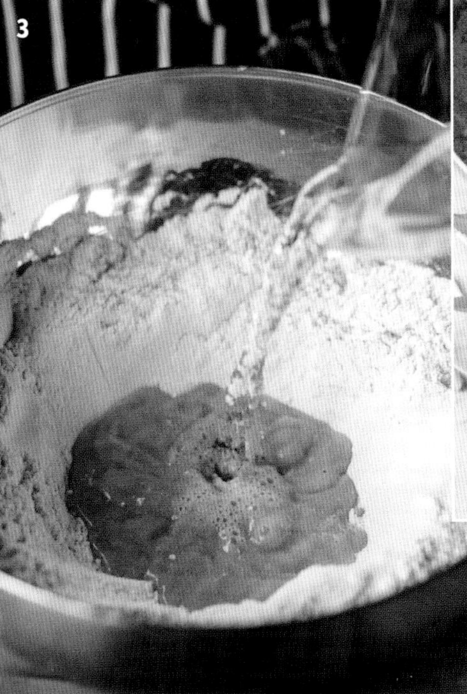

3 Mix the salt into the flour in the mixing bowl. Make a well in the middle of the flour. Pour in the bubbling yeast mixture and the rest of the warm water.

4 Mix everything with your hand, starting from the well and working your way out, incorporating the flour little by little.

5 Start to add the oil, a little at a time, and continue to mix with your hand.

6 When all the oil has been added, knead the ingredients until they form a dough which then starts to pull away from the sides of the bowl, about 8 minutes.

7 Chop the wild garlic and add most of it to the dough.

8 Work the dough by folding it over and pressing it with the heel of your hand; it will become firm and more elastic. (Alternatively, mix for 8 minutes in a stand mixer fitted with a dough hook.)

9 Form into a ball and put in a clean bowl. Cover with cling film or a clean tea towel and leave to prove somewhere quite warm for 1 hour.

10 After 1 hour, the dough should have doubled in size. At this point, your dough is ready to shape or put in a tin. Meanwhile, preheat the oven to 200°C/400°F/Gas 6 and grease an oven dish with olive oil.

11 Work the dough into the dish and make indents in the top with your fingertips. Sprinkle the top of the dough with sea salt and the remaining wild garlic.

12 Bake for about 25 minutes, until golden and cooked through.

MAKES 4 SMALL
OR 2 LARGE PIZZAS

18g fresh yeast
700ml warm water
1kg '00' strong white bread flour, plus extra for dusting
15g salt

Pizza

Dissolve the yeast in the warm water and leave for a few minutes to activate. Put the flour and salt into a large bowl and make a well in the centre. Add the yeasted water to the well and start to incorporate gradually to form a rough ball. Transfer the dough to a large, clean bowl, cover and leave to rise at room temperature for a long, slow prove, around 18 hours, until more than doubled in size and filled with lots of bubbles.

Tip the dough out onto the work surface and divide into 4 pieces (for 4 small pizzas) or 2 pieces (for 2 large pizzas). Shape each piece into a ball, put on floured baking tray(s) and cover. Leave to prove again for about 1 hour.

Preheat the oven to 240°C/475°F/Gas 9.

Gently start to shape one dough ball into a circle (or rectangle) with your fingertips, and put in back on the floured baking tray. Top your pizza dough with whatever sauce and toppings you desire and bake for about 10 minutes, depending on the thickness of your pizza, until the base of the pizza has a nice golden brown colour.

MAKES 20

40g fresh yeast
400ml lukewarm water
900g strong white bread flour
90g caster sugar
40g milk powder
15g salt
1 tsp bicarbonate of soda
100g rendered pork fat or melted lard

Steamed buns

Dissolve the yeast in the lukewarm water in the bowl of a stand mixer fitted with a dough hook and leave for a couple of minutes for the yeast to activate. Add the remaining ingredients and mix on low speed for 8 minutes. Cover the bowl and leave to prove at room temperature for 1 hour 15 minutes.

Remove the dough to the work surface and shape into 20 balls. Place on squares of baking parchment that will fit in a steamer and leave to prove for 30 minutes.

Steam on a high heat for 4–6 minutes.

MAKES 2 LOAVES

250g strong white bread flour,
  plus extra for dusting
250g wholemeal flour
100g fine oats
100g self-raising flour
3 tsp bicarbonate of soda
½ tsp salt
25g butter, softened
500ml buttermilk
150g maple syrup
50g honey

Maple syrup and buttermilk soda bread

Preheat the oven to 190°C/375°F/Gas 5.

Mix all the dry ingredients together in a large bowl, add the butter, buttermilk, maple syrup and honey to make a wet dough. Knead gently for a minute, then shape into 2 rectangles, 15 x 10cm. Place on a lightly floured baking tray and bake for 20–30 minutes, until golden brown.

MAKES ABOUT 15 LARGE
PRETZEL BUNS

260ml milk
260ml water
30g runny honey
42g fresh yeast
1kg plain flour
80g butter
20g salt

COOKING WATER

5 litres water
45g bicarbonate of soda
50g runny honey

FOR BAKING

Oil, for greasing
Milk, for coating

Pretzel buns

Warm the milk and water together slightly (not too hot) and add the honey and yeast. Put the flour, butter and salt into the bowl of a stand mixer fitted with a dough hook, add the yeasty liquid and mix for 8 minutes on medium speed until a smooth dough forms. Cover the bowl with cling film and leave to prove at room temperature for 2 hours.

Take the dough out, briefly knead by hand, then shape into a large ball. Roll the ball into a long log shape and cut pieces of dough each weighing 100g. Shape each piece into a ball and press down with the palm of your hand to flatten into a bun. Lightly oil a baking tray and place the buns on the tray, leaving a 5-cm gap between each. Loosely cover the tray with cling film and leave to prove again for 1 hour.

Preheat the oven to 190°C/375°F/Gas 5.

Bring the cooking water to the boil in a large pan or stockpot and add the bicarbonate of soda and honey. Working in batches, add the buns and boil for 2 minutes, flipping them over after halfway through. Remove with a slotted spoon and let drain for a few minutes.

Dip each bun in milk to coat completely and transfer back to the oiled baking tray. Score the buns across the top with a razor or sharp knife, then bake until dark brown.

MAKES 15 LARGE BAGELS

355ml warm water
75g caster sugar
45ml vegetable oil
18g fresh yeast
1 egg, beaten
15g milk powder
1kg plain flour
12g salt

COOKING WATER

6 litres water
80g honey

FOR BAKING

Oil, for greasing
1 egg, lightly beaten
Sesame or poppy seeds, or sea salt, for sprinkling

Bagels

Put the water, sugar, oil, yeast, egg and milk powder into the bowl of a stand mixer fitted with a dough attachment. Leave to rest for a few minutes until the yeast has activated, then add the flour and salt and mix on low speed for 1 minute. Increase the speed to medium and mix for a further 6–7 minutes until you have a smooth dough. Cover the bowl and leave to prove at room temperature for 1 hour.

Oil a baking tray and set aside. Take the dough out and knead by hand for 1 minute. Divide the dough into pieces each weighing 100g and keep them covered. Roll each piece of dough into a ball, then make a hole in the centre, stretching it apart to form a bagel shape. Put each shaped bagel onto the oiled tray, spaced apart, and cover lightly with cling film. Leave to prove for 40 minutes–1 hour.

Preheat the oven to 180°C/350°F/Gas 4.

Bring the cooking water and honey to the boil in a large pan or stockpot and, working in batches, drop the bagels into the water. Boil for 2 minutes, flipping them over halfway through. Use a slotted spoon to remove them to the oiled tray. Brush each bagel with the beaten egg and sprinkle with sesame seeds, poppy seeds or sea salt, as you prefer. Bake the bagels for about 20 minutes, flipping them over halfway through baking.

MAKES 9–12

300ml milk
20g caster sugar
30g unsalted butter
15g active dried yeast
500g strong white bread flour
10g salt
1 large egg
Oil, for greasing
Softened butter, for greasing and topping
Demerara sugar, for sprinkling

FILLING

150g walnuts, chopped
150g unsalted butter, softened
150g granulated sugar
50g maple syrup

Walnut and maple Chelsea buns

Put the milk, caster sugar and butter in a saucepan and heat gently to just melt the butter. When the milk has cooled to just warm, add the yeast and leave for a few minutes to activate it.

Put the flour and salt into the bowl of a stand mixer with a dough hook attachment and add the egg and the milk mixture. Mix on low speed for 1 minute until combined, then turn up to medium speed and mix for 10–12 minutes until you have a strong, smooth and elastic dough. Transfer the dough to a lightly oiled bowl, cover and leave to prove for 1 hour, or until doubled in size.

Meanwhile, for the filling, preheat the oven to 180°C/350°F/Gas 4. Roast the walnuts for about 10 minutes, turning them now and then. Leave to cool. Beat the butter until creamy, then fold in the cooled walnuts, sugar and maple syrup.

Take the dough out and roll it into a rectangle about 1cm thick. Spread the entire surface with the walnut and maple filling, then roll up the dough from the long side into a log. Cut the log into thick rounds, about 5cm thick. Brush a baking tin with butter and sprinkle with some Demerara sugar. Put the buns in the tin, cut-side up, leaving about a 1-cm space between each one. Put a dab of butter and a sprinkle of sugar on each bun, loosely cover the tin with cling film and leave to prove again for 30 minutes. Bake the buns for 20–25 minutes.

For alternative fillings, see page 213.

MAKES ABOUT 20

Pizza dough (see page 126)
200g caster sugar
50g ground cinnamon
Vegetable or rapeseed oil, for deep-frying

Fried dough (beavertails)

Cut the dough (after its second proving) into approximately 80-g pieces and shape each one into an oval shape (like a beaver's tail!). Mix the sugar and cinnamon together in a large bowl.

Heat the oil to 170°C in a deep-fryer or other suitable deep, heavy pan, and fry each piece of dough until lightly golden brown on both sides. Remove and drain on kitchen paper. Toss in the cinnamon sugar until completely covered, then serve immediately.

1

Rough puff pastry

Making traditional puff pastry at home requires some time, and although it yields great results, a rough puff pastry is a great alternative, producing very good results in less time. The ingredients are the same, so you'll still have a wonderful buttery flavour, however the rise on the pastry will be a little bit less than the traditional dough.

1 Tip 250g plain flour onto the work surface. Add 250g cubed, cold unsalted butter.

2 Start to rub the butter into the flour with your fingers.

3 Mix together until you have little chunks of mixture. Mix in ½ tsp fine sea salt. Do not overwork the dough, or it will become tough and the butter will get too soft and start to seep.

4 Make a well in the middle. Gradually add 150ml cold water to the well – about a third at a time – and mix in with your fingertips. (You can use a food processor with a paddle attachment to do this.)

5 Bring together to form a dough.

6 Once the dough comes together, dust it and the work surface lightly with flour.

7 Roll out into a large rectangle.

8 Fold into a book fold (fold the sides into the middle and close like a book).

9 Turn the dough 90 degrees, roll out again into a small rectangle and do another book fold.

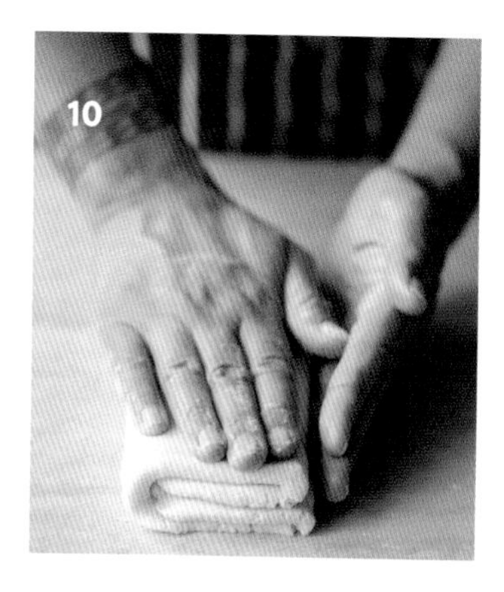

10 Fold in the middle. Wrap in cling film and refrigerate for 30 minutes.

11 Repeat Steps 9 and 10 twice more, with a 30-minute rest in between, then the pastry is ready to use. Makes about 650g.

MAKES ABOUT 20

½ quantity Rough Puff Pastry (see pages 134–137)
200g granulated sugar
2 tbsp ground cardamom

Sweet cardamom palmiers

Roll the pastry out to 3mm thick and cut into 4 rectangular strips. Mix the sugar and ground cardamom together and sprinkle some of it over the pastry strips. Fold each pastry strip in half lengthways and roll out again to the same sized rectangles.

Sprinkle heavily with more of the sugar mixture, then roll the short side of each strip in towards the centre, keeping it tight as you roll. Roll the other short side in towards the centre in the same way, so they meet. Press the two sides together then wrap in cling film and put into the freezer to set.

Preheat the oven to 180°C/350°F/Gas 4.

Remove the frozen pastry and leave to thaw for 10 minutes, then cut into 1-cm thick slices. Toss in the remaining sugar mixture until completely covered and put on an unlined baking tray. Cook for 15 minutes, flipping them over halfway through cooking. Remove from the baking tray immediately and serve.

MAKES 30–40

600ml whole milk
2 cloves
½ onion
1 fresh or dried bay leaf
80g unsalted butter, plus extra for the pan
80g plain flour
1 tbsp English mustard powder
200g Comté cheese or good aged Cheddar, grated, plus extra for the pan
Rough Puff Pastry (see pages 134–137)
12 slices of prosciutto or Bayonne ham

Prosciutto and cheese bites

Put the milk, cloves, onion and bay leaf into a saucepan and slowly bring to the boil. Remove from the heat and set aside to infuse.

Melt the butter in a saucepan, then whisk in the flour and mustard powder. Cook on a low heat for a few minutes, then strain the milk and gradually add it to the roux. Cook for 5–6 minutes, whisking all the time, until the flour has been cooked out. Add the cheese, mix well and leave to cool.

Preheat the oven to 190°C/375°F/Gas 5.

Roll out the pastry into a large rectangle, 30 x 40cm. Spread the cooled cheese mixture over the entire surface of the pastry. Lay the ham on top, covering the whole area. Tightly roll the pastry up from the long side into a log and cut into slices about 4cm thick.

Brush a large ovenproof frying pan or oven dish with butter and sprinkle with some more grated cheese. Fit the buns into the pan, leaving about 1cm space between each. Sprinkle more cheese over the top and bake in the oven for 25 minutes, until golden brown.

MAKES ABOUT 20

8 sun-dried tomatoes, drained and finely chopped
100g tomato purée
½ quantity Rough Puff Pastry (see pages 134–137)
200g pitted green olives, finely chopped

Savoury tomato and olive palmiers

Mix the sun-dried tomatoes and tomato purée together and set aside.

Roll the pastry out to a large square 3mm thick and cut into 4 rectangular strips. Spread the tomato mixture onto the pastry rectangles to cover entirely, and sprinkle on the chopped green olives.

Roll the short side of each strip in towards the centre, keeping it tight as you roll. Roll the other short side in towards the centre in the same way, so they meet. Press the two sides together, then wrap in cling film and put in the freezer to set.

Preheat the oven to 180°C/350°F/Gas 4.

Remove the frozen pastry and leave to thaw for 10 minutes, then cut into 1-cm thick slices. Put on an unlined baking tray and cook for 15 minutes, flipping them over halfway through the cooking. Remove from the baking tray immediately and serve.

SERVES 6

½ quantity Rough Puff Pastry (see pages 134–137)
Frangipane (see pages 182–183)
12 ripe figs
50g butter, melted
30g Demerara sugar
Sprinkling of icing sugar

Fig 'tarte fine'

Preheat the oven to 190°C/375°F/Gas 5.

Roll the pastry out to a rectangle about 3mm thick (setting a small piece of pastry to one side) and put on a baking tray lined with baking parchment. Prick the pastry at intervals using a fork. Pipe a thin layer of Frangipane over the pastry, leaving a 2-cm border around the edge. Put the reserved piece of pastry on a separate, lined baking tray.

Cut the figs vertically into thick slices and arrange in neat overlapping layers to cover the pastry, then fold in the edges of the pastry. Brush all over with the melted butter and sprinkle with the sugar, then bake both trays in the oven 20–25 minutes until cooked.

Take the baked little piece of pastry and crumble finely into a pan with a sprinkling of icing sugar. Cook, stirring, until the sugar has caramelised on the pieces of pastry. Serve the tart warm, sprinkled with the caramelised pastry crumbs, ice cream and honey.

SERVES 6

½ quantity Rough Puff Pastry
(see pages 134–137)
4 medium eggs, plus 2 egg yolks,
in separate bowls
300ml milk
Pinch each of sea salt, freshly ground black
pepper and grated nutmeg
200g mature Cheddar, grated

LEFTOVERS

10 'pigs in blankets'
Large handful of stuffing
Handful of roast pumpkin and parsnips

Christmas leftovers quiche

Preheat the oven to 200°C/400°F/Gas 6. Line a 20 x 30-cm oven dish with the pastry and pierce at intervals using a fork. Line the pastry with baking parchment and fill with baking beans or uncooked rice. Transfer to the oven for 15 minutes, or until golden brown.

Remove the beans and parchment and brush the pastry base with a little of the egg yolks, then return to the oven for 1 minute. Remove and set aside to cool. Reduce the oven temperature to 160°C/325°F/Gas 3.

Mix the whole eggs and remaining yolks with the milk, adding the salt, pepper and nutmeg. Sprinkle some of the grated cheese over the pastry base to cover. Roughly break up the leftovers and distribute over the cheese. Place the dish on an oven tray and pour the egg mixture into the case, then sprinkle over the remaining cheese.

Bake in the oven for about 45–50 minutes, or until just set to the touch. Leave to cool before serving.

Choux pastry

Quick and easy to make, choux pastry is the perfect vehicle for many sweet and savoury dishes – amazing chocolate éclairs or hot cheese gougères, for example. This pastry is impressive and delicious.

1 Place 65ml water, 60ml whole milk, 50g cubed unsalted butter and a pinch of fine sea salt in a large saucepan on a medium heat.

2 Bring to the boil, then turn down the heat, add 75g plain flour in one go and beat in with a wooden spoon to form a dough.

3 Turn off the heat and continue to beat until the dough is cooled to room temperature. (Alternatively, you can place it in a mixer fitted with a paddle attachment at this stage and beat until cool.)

4 Add 2 medium eggs, one at a time, and beat again with the spoon (or in the mixer) until well combined.

5 You should have a thick, shiny paste that is firm and pipeable. Makes enough for about 30 choux buns.

MAKES ABOUT 25

Choux Pastry (see pages 146–147, and method below)
20g squid ink

SPICED CRAB

300g crab meat (see pages 70–71)
1 tbsp finely chopped chives
2 tbsp Coriander and Lime Mayonnaise (see page 110)
1 tbsp finely chopped red chilli (deseeded)
Pinch of smoked paprika

Squid-ink choux with spiced crab

Preheat the oven to 200°C/400°F/Gas 6.

When making the Choux Pastry, mix in the squid ink after the eggs have been beaten in.

Fill a piping bag with the pastry and pipe medium rounds of it onto baking trays lined with baking parchment, and bake for 8 minutes, then reduce the oven temperature to 180°C/350°F/Gas 4 and bake for a further 25 minutes. Transfer the choux to a wire rack to cool.

Mix all the spiced crab ingredients together in a bowl.

When the choux buns are cool, cut a small lid off each, fill with the crab mixture and replace the lids. These make great little pre-meal snacks.

SERVES 8–10

250ml double cream
30g icing sugar
1 vanilla pod, split lengthways and seeds scraped out
Crème Pâtissière (see page 213)
Choux Pastry (see pages 146–147)

Cream custard choux slice

Whip the cream, icing sugar and vanilla seeds together, then fold through the cooled Crème Pâtissière. Keep refrigerated until needed.

Preheat the oven to 200°C/400°F/Gas 6. Divide the choux mixture in half and spread evenly to a thickness of about 5mm onto 2 baking trays lined with baking parchment. Bake in the oven for 10 minutes, then reduce the oven temperature to 180°C/350°F/Gas 4 and cook for a further 20–25 minutes. Leave the choux layers to cool on a wire rack.

Pipe or spread the cream mixture onto one of the cooled choux layers and place the second on top. Press down firmly and chill for 30 minutes.

Cut into portions and serve with salted chocolate caramel sauce.

SERVES 2

2 large baking potatoes, such as King Edward, unpeeled
150g bone marrow
Choux Pastry (see pages 146–147), warm
300ml sunflower or vegetable oil, for deep-frying
Sea salt and freshly ground black pepper

Bone marrow pommes dauphines

Cook the potatoes whole in plenty of salted water until tender. Drain and return to the pan to dry out for 1–2 minutes. Leave until cool enough to handle.

Meanwhile, place the bone marrow in a pan of cold salted water and gently bring to a simmer. Poach for 2 minutes, then drain on kitchen paper and refrigerate.

Scoop out the middles of the potatoes and pass twice through a potato ricer. Mix with the warm Choux Pastry and season with a little salt and pepper.

Chop up the marrow and add to the potato and choux mixture. Shape into your desired shapes, such as quenelles or round balls. Store on a sheet of greaseproof paper in the fridge until needed.

Heat the oil to 160°C in a deep-fryer or other suitable deep, heavy pan. Cook the pommes dauphines in the hot oil until they turn golden brown and float to the surface, then drain on kitchen paper and serve immediately.

MAKES 12 LARGE GOUGÈRES

Choux Pastry (see pages 146–147,
and method below)
200g Gruyère, grated
50g English mustard
4 large gherkins, sliced
12 pastrami slices
Small bunch of watercress

Cheese puff and pastrami sandwiches

Preheat the oven to 200°C/400°F/Gas 6.

When making the Choux Pastry, mix the grated cheese in well after the eggs have been beaten in. Use a large kitchen spoon to scoop mounds of the choux mixture onto a baking tray lined with baking parchment.

Bake for 10 minutes, then reduce the oven temperature to 180°C/350°F/Gas 4 and bake for a further 25 minutes. Transfer to a wire rack to cool.

When cool, cut each in half and spread the mustard inside. Add some sliced gherkin and pastrami, then finish with watercress and serve.

MAKES 25

Choux Pastry (see pages 146–147), warm
Lemon Curd (see page 212)
½ quantity Italian Meringue
(see pages 156–157)

Lemon curd profiteroles

Preheat the oven to 200°C/400°F/Gas 6. Fill a piping bag with the Choux Pastry and pipe small rounds of it onto baking trays lined with baking parchment. Bake for 8 minutes, then reduce the oven temperature to 180°C/350°F/Gas 4 and bake for a further 15 minutes. Transfer to a wire rack to cool.

Make a small hole in the bases of the cooled profiteroles and pipe in the Lemon Curd to fill. Place in the fridge until needed. To serve, pipe some Italian Meringue onto each profiterole and glaze just very briefly with a kitchen blowtorch or under a very hot grill.

Italian meringue

Italian meringues are made from whisking a syrup cooked to 121°C into egg whites. It is a very versatile meringue and once you have grasped the method, you will be able to create countless masterpieces of your own. The key to getting it right is to a) to make sure you have whisked your egg whites before adding the syrup; b) to let the syrup settle a minute after reaching 121°C before pouring into the whisked egg whites; c) to whisk for 5 minutes to cool before using.

1 Put 60ml water, 240g caster sugar and 15g liquid glucose (optional, to make the meringue more stable) in a saucepan on a medium heat and bring slowly to the boil, brushing down any crystals forming on the sides using a wet pastry brush. Place a thermometer in the liquid, increase the heat and cook, without stirring, to 121°C.

2 Whisk 4 medium egg whites to stiff peaks. Slowly add 30g caster sugar while whisking, to help stabilise the meringue.

3 After the syrup has settled off the heat for a minute, pour it into the meringue in a steady stream, whisking constantly.

4 Continue to whisk until the mixture has cooled, then either use immediately or store in an airtight container in the fridge.

4

SERVES 10–12

SWEET PASTRY

250g butter, softened
150g icing sugar
4 large egg yolks, plus 1 extra, mixed with a little water
500g plain flour
Pinch of salt

FILLING

1 small pineapple, peeled, cored and diced
260g egg yolks (about 13 eggs)
150ml pineapple juice
60g caster sugar
600ml whipping cream
1 tsp rapeseed oil

ITALIAN MERINGUE

40ml water
175g caster sugar for the syrup, plus 25g for the egg whites
100g egg whites (about 2½ eggs)

Pineapple meringue pie

For the sweet pastry, beat the butter and icing sugar together until pale, then beat in the egg yolks one at a time. Gradually mix in the flour and salt, then rest in the fridge for 20 minutes. Preheat the oven to 180°C/350°F/Gas 4.

Roll out the pastry and use to line a baking tin 21cm square and 6cm deep. Trim off the excess pastry and prick the base with a fork. Line with baking parchment and fill with baking beans or uncooked rice. Bake for 11–15 minutes, then remove the parchment and beans and continue to cook until golden, another 10 minutes. Remove from the oven and brush with the extra yolk and water mixture. Place back in the oven for 1 minute, then remove and leave to cool. Reduce the oven temperature to 150°C/300°F/Gas 2.

For the filling, put the pineapple dice into a non-stick frying pan and roast over a medium heat until golden. Spread evenly over the cooked pastry case. Whisk the egg yolks, pineapple juice and sugar together in a bowl. Heat the cream to just warmed, then pour into the yolk mixture, whisking. Pour the filling into the cooked base over the pineapple and return to the oven for 50–55 minutes, until set. Leave to cool completely.

Meanwhile, make an Italian meringue with the water, sugar and egg whites (see pages 156–157) and pipe on top of the pineapple filling. Glaze the meringue under a hot grill or with a blowtorch and serve cold or at room temperature.

SERVES 6

Lemon Curd (see page 212)
1 punnet of physalis (cape gooseberries)
Handful of wild strawberries
Micro basil

ITALIAN MERINGUE

50ml water
125g caster sugar
3 egg whites
10g liquid glucose
Cracked black pepper

Lemon and peppered meringue

Preheat the oven to 110°C/225°F/Gas ¼. Make an Italian meringue with the water, sugar, egg whites and liquid glucose (see pages 156–157, but use all the sugar for the syrup and don't put any directly in the egg whites), then divide the meringue in half, placing one half in a bowl and the other in a piping bag. Pipe some thin lines of meringue onto a baking tray lined with baking parchment and sprinkle with cracked black pepper. Bake until dry, about 1–1½ hours. (You could alternatively leave them in the oven overnight on 90°C/195°F, which I find best.)

Spread some of the reserved meringue onto a plate using a flat spatula. Use a kitchen blowtorch or grill to gently colour the meringue. Pipe some Lemon Curd around the meringue and decorate with the physalis, strawberries, micro basil and the cooked meringue.

SERVES 6

2 tbsp hazelnuts
6 slices of brioche, 1.5cm thick
6 tbsp Nutella

NUTELLA ICE CREAM

400ml milk
100ml double cream
2 vanilla pods, split lengthways
6 medium egg yolks
60g caster sugar
½ tsp natural vanilla extract
150g Nutella

ITALIAN MERINGUE

50ml water
125g caster sugar
3 egg whites

Baked Alaska with Nutella ice cream

Preheat the oven to 190°C/375°F/Gas 5. Spread the hazelnuts out on a baking tray and toast for 5 minutes. Leave to cool a little, then crush and set aside.

For the Nutella ice cream, make a crème anglaise with the milk, cream, vanilla pods, egg yolks, sugar and vanilla extract (see pages 168–169). Pass the thickened custard through a conical strainer onto the Nutella, in a bowl, and stir until well mixed. Churn in an ice-cream machine for about 20 minutes. Line a small oval bowl or mould with cling film, press the ice cream inside and freeze to set.

Make an Italian meringue with the water, sugar and egg whites (see pages 156–157, but use all the sugar for the syrup and don't put any directly in the egg whites).

If you don't have a blowtorch, heat the grill to high. Arrange the slices of brioche in a single layer on a baking tray so that they form a shape 1cm larger than the base of the mould. Spread with Nutella. Remove the set ice cream from the mould, peeling off the cling film, and turn out on top of the brioche slices.

Pipe the Italian meringue around and over the ice cream and, working quickly, very briefly glaze under a hot grill or with a kitchen blowtorch. Sprinkle with the crushed toasted hazelnuts and serve immediately.

MAKES ABOUT 10 TARTLETS

Rough Puff Pastry (see pages 134–137)
Crème Pâtissière (see page 213)
Selection of soft fruits, such as raspberries, strawberries, mangos and kiwis, halved or sliced as appropriate

MANGO ITALIAN MERINGUE

60g mango purée
125g caster sugar
3 egg whites

Fruit tartlets with meringue

Preheat the oven to 180°C/350°F/Gas 4. Roll out the puff pastry to 5mm thick. Cut out individual rounds of pastry and use to line as many 10-cm tartlet tins as you can. Line with baking parchment and baking beans or uncooked rice and bake for about 10 minutes. Now remove the parchment and baking beans and bake again for 5–10 minutes until golden. Set aside to cool.

For the mango Italian meringue, put the mango purée and sugar into a saucepan and bring to the boil. Meanwhile, whisk the egg whites to stiff peaks. Pour the hot mango mixture in a steady stream onto the whisked whites, whisking constantly as you would for an Italian meringue (see pages 156–157). Continue whisking for 5 minutes, until cooled.

To assemble the tartlets, spread some crème pâtissière into each pastry case and fill with a selection of fruit, then pipe the mango Italian meringue on top, in a tall mound.

Pistachio parfait with thyme-soaked fruits

SERVES 6

40g pistachios
40g caster sugar
140ml whipping cream, semi whipped
Seeds of 1 large pomegranate
1 punnet of physalis (cape gooseberries), quartered

SHORTBREAD BISCUITS

200g butter
100g caster sugar
300g plain flour
Pinch of salt

ITALIAN MERINGUE

125g caster sugar
3 egg whites

THYME SYRUP

200ml water
200g caster sugar
7 long thyme sprigs
1 star anise
1 cinnamon stick
1 tbsp lime juice

Preheat the oven to 180°C/350°F/Gas 4. Line a baking tray with baking parchment.

For the shortbread biscuits, cream the butter and sugar together, then stir in the flour and salt until combined. Press or roll out to 1.5cm thick on the lined baking tray. Bake for about 20 minutes or until just golden. When still warm, cut into your preferred shapes.

For the parfait, line 6 individual moulds with baking parchment to come 3–4cm above the rim. Spread the pistachios out on a baking tray and toast in the oven for 5 minutes. Make a caramel with the sugar (see pages 200–201) and pour over the toasted pistachios, then crush and set aside.

Make an Italian meringue with the sugar and egg whites (see pages 156–157) then fold in the crushed pistachio caramel and semi-whipped cream. Transfer to the prepared moulds and put in the freezer for at least 1½–2 hours.

For the thyme syrup, bring the water, sugar, thyme and spices to the boil in a saucepan. Set aside to cool, then add the lime juice. Pour the syrup over the pomegranate seeds and physalis and leave to soak for 5 minutes, then remove the thyme, star anise and cinnamon stick.

To serve, place a shortbread biscuit on each serving plate. Unmould the parfaits, peel off the parchment and place a parfait on top of each biscuit. Top with a second biscuit and spoon the thyme soaked fruits with their syrup onto the plates.

SERVES 10

400g very ripe peaches, halved and pitted
175g caster sugar
2 tsp lime juice
400g whipping cream, semi whipped
50g confit ginger in syrup, chopped
into small pieces
100g lime marmalade, plus extra to serve
Finely grated lime zest, to decorate

ITALIAN MERINGUE

50ml water
125g caster sugar
60g egg whites (about 1½ eggs)

Iced peach, lime and ginger soufflés

Line the insides of 10 x 8-cm chef's rings or cups with baking parchment to come 3–4cm above the rims and place on a flat baking tray.

Blitz the peaches with the sugar and strain into a large bowl, then stir in the lime juice.

Make an Italian meringue with the water, sugar and egg whites (see pages 156–157, but use all the sugar for the syrup and don't put any directly in the egg whites).

Fold the semi-whipped cream into the peach mixture, then fold in the chopped ginger, followed by the Italian meringue. Very gently fold in the marmalade so you can see it marbled through the mixture.

Fill each lined ring or cup with the mixture and place in the freezer to set. When set, remove from the rings or cups, peel off the baking parchment. Serve with an extra spoonful of lime marmalade and some grated lime zest.

Crème anglaise

Crème anglaise is a versatile sweet, light custard sauce. Often flavoured with vanilla, it can transform a dish – the perfect partner to a warm bread pudding, or enriched with more egg yolks and double cream, the base for a great vanilla ice cream.

1 Whisk 60g caster sugar, 6 medium egg yolks and ½ tsp natural vanilla extract together in a bowl. Pour 300ml whole milk and 200ml double cream into a heavy-based saucepan, add 2 vanilla pods split lengthways, and bring to the boil on a medium heat.

2 Remove the pan from the heat and start to pour a little of it slowly into the bowl with the egg yolk mixture, whisking constantly to prevent the eggs from scrambling.

3 When you've added just a little of the hot milk from the pan, pour all the mixture from the bowl back into the pan and whisk to incorporate.

4 Cook on a medium-low heat for about 5 minutes, until thick enough to coat the back of a wooden spoon (or to 82°C). Strain into a clean bowl and chill over a bowl of iced water unless serving straight away. Makes about 500ml.

SERVES 4

75ml whole milk
380ml double cream
2 blood oranges, peel only
75g Demerara sugar
5 egg yolks

COMPOTE

3 blood oranges
40g caster sugar, plus extra for glazing

Blood orange crèmes brûlées

This is my favourite brûlée recipe that came about one weekend on request from my husband and daughter. We had a few blood oranges and this is what we came up with.

For the compote, finely zest one of the blood oranges and set the zest aside. Peel the remaining 2 oranges and the zest one, and chop the orange flesh into pieces, removing the seeds. Place in a small saucepan, add the grated zest and caster sugar and stew to a thick compote consistency. Keep chilled until needed. Preheat the oven to 110°C/225°F/Gas ¼.

Pour the milk and cream into a saucepan, add the orange peel and bring to the boil. Meanwhile, whisk the Demerara sugar and yolks together in a bowl. Strain the hot milk and cream mixture and pour onto the egg yolk mixture, whisking as you pour.

Place some of the chilled compote in 4 gratin moulds and smooth out to cover the base of each. Put the dishes onto a baking tray to catch any spills. Pour the custard mixture into each and bake for 35 minutes. Remove and leave at room temperature to set.

To serve, sprinkle a layer of caster sugar on top and use a kitchen blowtorch to glaze to a golden brown.

SERVES 4–5

600ml whole milk
400ml whipping cream
1 vanilla pod, split lengthways
3 cinnamon sticks
1 tsp grated nutmeg, plus extra to serve
6 eggs, separated
140g caster sugar, plus 2 tbsp for the egg whites
200ml dark rum

Spiced eggnog

Pour the milk and cream into a saucepan, scrape the vanilla seeds into the mixture, and add the vanilla pod, cinnamon sticks and nutmeg. Slowly bring to the boil, then remove from the heat, cover with cling film and set aside for 10 minutes to infuse.

Meanwhile, put the egg yolks and sugar into the bowl of a stand mixer fitted with a whisk attachment and whisk until thick ribbons form.

Strain the milk and cream mixture and gradually add to the egg yolk mixture, whisking slowly as you do so. Add the rum and keep in the fridge until needed.

When ready to serve, whisk the egg whites with the 2 tbsp sugar until soft peaks form. Blend the eggnog mixture to lighten, then fold in the egg whites, grate some fresh nutmeg over the top and serve.

SERVES 4

100ml Guinness
2x 80ml Fever-Tree ginger ales

GINGER ICE CREAM

300ml whole milk
200ml double cream
1 vanilla pod, split lengthways
6 medium egg yolks
65g caster sugar
½ tsp natural vanilla extract
2 tbsp ground ginger

GINGER CAKE AND CRUMBLE

225g plain flour
2 tsp ground ginger
Pinch of ground cinnamon
Pinch of mixed spice
Pinch of salt
85g butter, plus extra for greasing
225g golden syrup
55g Demerara sugar
1 egg
Icing sugar, for dusting
20ml milk
1 small, firm pear, peeled and diced
1 piece of confit ginger in syrup, diced

GINGER CREAM

125g crème fraîche
125ml double cream
10ml syrup from jar of confit ginger in syrup

Guinness and ginger float

For the ginger ice cream, pour the milk and cream into a heavy-based saucepan, scrape in the vanilla seeds and bring to the boil. Meanwhile, whisk the yolks and sugar together in a bowl. Pour the hot cream and milk mixture over the yolk mixture and mix, then pour back into the pan and cook on a medium-low until thick (or until it reaches 82°C). Remove from the heat, strain and stir in the vanilla extract and ground ginger. Chill, then churn in an ice-cream machine until set.

For the ginger cake and crumble, preheat the oven to 170°C/325°F/Gas 3. Mix the flour, spices and salt together in a bowl. Melt the butter, syrup and sugar together in a pan. Whisk the egg and milk together in a separate bowl. Add the wet ingredients to the dry and mix. Pour into a greased, shallow baking tray and bake for 8–10 minutes, until cooked. Leave the oven on. (This will make more cake than you need for this recipe, but extra cake is never a bad thing!)

Cut off 100g of the ginger cake and roughly chop. Dust with icing sugar and toast in the oven for 2–3 minutes. Set aside.

For the ginger cream, whisk the ingredients together and chill.

To serve, mix the pear with the confit ginger and toss the toasted cake through the pear mixture to make the crumble. Place some crumble mixture in the bottom of a glass serving bowl. Place a scoop of ginger ice cream on top, then a spoonful of ginger cream. Pour in the Guinness, then the ginger ale. Sprinkle more crumble on top and serve.

Cherry and amaretti trifle

SERVES 8–10

AMARETTI BISCUITS

250g ground almonds
250g caster sugar
125g egg whites
30ml amaretto liqueur
1 tbsp almond extract

CHERRY AND KIRSCH JELLY

250ml Kirsch
Stock Syrup (see page 212)
1 star anise
1 cinnamon stick
3 crushed cardamom pods
4 bronze gelatine sheets

VANILLA CUSTARD

1 vanilla pod, split lengthways
100ml whole milk
400ml double cream
60g caster sugar
6 large egg yolks

CHERRY COMPOTE

250g fresh cherries, pitted and halved
100g cherries, soaked for 30 minutes in Kirsch
60g caster sugar

WHIPPED CREAM

1 vanilla pod, split lengthways
500ml whipping cream
30g caster sugar

TO ASSEMBLE

500ml Marsala wine
2 tbsp caster sugar
Handful of fresh cherries, pitted and halved

For the amaretti biscuits, preheat the oven to 160°C/325°F/Gas 3 and line 2 baking trays with baking parchment. Mix the ground almonds with half the sugar in a bowl. Whisk the egg whites to soft peaks, then whisk in the remaining sugar a little at a time, to make a meringue. Whisk in the amaretto and almond extract, then gently fold the meringue mixture into the almond and sugar mixture until you have a thick paste. Put the mixture into a piping bag and pipe medium-sized circles or fingers onto the baking trays. Bake for 25–30 minutes, until golden brown. Leave to cool on the trays, then store in an airtight container until ready to use.

For the cherry and kirsch jelly, put the Kirsch, Stock Syrup and spices into a saucepan and bring to the boil. Take off the heat and let sit for 10 minutes. Put the gelatine sheets into iced water and, once soft, squeeze out the excess water. Mix the gelatine into the hot liquid, then strain through a fine-mesh sieve. Line a tray at least 2cm deep with cling film and pour the Kirsch liquid in, to about 2cm deep. Put into the fridge to set.

Continued on page 176...

For the vanilla custard, scrape the seeds from the vanilla pod and put both the seeds and pod in a saucepan with the milk and cream. Slowly bring to the boil and set aside. Whisk the sugar and egg yolks together in a bowl, then whisk in the hot milk mixture. Pour back into the saucepan and heat gently, whisking until it thickens. Cool and refrigerate until needed.

For the cherry compote, put the cherries and sugar into a saucepan and cook until the cherries have softened and released their juices, then remove from the heat and cool.

For the whipped cream, scrape the vanilla seeds from the pod into a bowl with the whipping cream and sugar. Whip the cream until soft peaks form.

To assemble the trifle, choose either individual glasses or a large glass bowl to build your trifle. Put the Marsala and sugar into a mixing bowl. Start by piling a layer of the cherry compote in the bottom of your glasses or trifle bowl. Soak a few amaretti biscuits in the Marsala, then place on top of the compote. Cut some cubes of cherry jelly and scatter over the amaretti, then cover with some of the custard and whipped cream. Add another layer of compote, soaked biscuits, jelly and custard. Finally, pipe a thick layer of whipped cream on top, then crush a few amaretti biscuits and sprinkle on top with the fresh cherries.

SERVES 8

8 Williams or Conference pears, peeled and cored
Chopped candied walnuts

WALNUT ICE CREAM

250ml single cream
250ml whole milk
6 egg yolks
120g caster sugar
150g walnuts, toasted and chopped

SABLÉ BISCUITS

500g plain flour
2 pinches of salt
200g caster sugar
500g butter, softened
2 tsp vanilla extract
4 egg yolks
1 tbsp double cream

WHITE WINE POACHING LIQUID

250ml white wine
400g caster sugar
1 cinnamon stick
1 vanilla pod, split lengthways

RED WINE POACHING LIQUID

250ml strong red wine
140g caster sugar
1 cinnamon stick
Zest and juice of 1 lemon

Red- and white-wine poached pears with walnut ice cream

For the walnut ice cream, bring the cream and milk to the boil in a saucepan. Meanwhile, whisk the egg yolks and sugar in a bowl until combined. Gradually whisk in the milk and cream mixture, then pour back into the saucepan and cook gently to thicken slightly. Add the walnuts, stir and leave to steep overnight in the fridge.

The next day, strain the ice cream mixture through a fine-mesh sieve and churn in an ice-cream machine until set.

Continued overleaf...

For the sablé biscuits, preheat the oven to 180°C/350°F/Gas 4 and line 2 baking trays with baking parchment.

Sift the flour into a bowl and stir in the salt and sugar. Stir in the butter, vanilla, egg yolks and cream, but don't overwork the mixture. Cover and rest in the fridge for 30 minutes. Roll out the chilled dough until 5mm thick, then stamp out rounds and place on the baking trays. Bake for 8–10 minutes, then leave to cool on the trays.

Bring the 2 poaching liquids to the boil in separate pans. Poach 4 of the pears in the white wine mixture and the other 4 in the red wine solution for 8–10 minutes, until cooked but still firm, then leave to cool in the poaching liquid.

When cool, take the pears out of the pans and put the red poaching liquor on a high heat. Bring to the boil and reduce to a syrup.

To serve, thinly slice the poached pears and arrange on plates with the walnut ice cream. Crumble the sablé biscuits over the top and decorate with the chopped candied walnuts. Decorate with drops of the poaching syrup.

SERVES 6

Rough Puff Pastry (see pages 134–137)
Handful of pistachio nuts, finely chopped

DULCE DE LECHE GANACHE

120ml whole milk
360ml double cream
3 large egg yolks
290g dulce de leche or similar chocolate, melted

TO SERVE

80g fresh raspberries
Icing sugar, for dusting

Dulce de leche ganache with raspberries

Preheat the oven to 200°C/400°F/Gas 6 and line a baking tray with baking parchment. Set aside another sheet of parchment and a second baking tray.

Roll out the Rough Puff Pastry until about 5mm thick. Lay on the lined baking tray and put another sheet of parchment on top. Cover with the second baking tray. Bake for 20 minutes, or until golden brown and crispy, then leave to cool.

For the dulce de leche ganache, pour the milk and cream into a saucepan and bring to a gentle boil. Meanwhile, gently whisk the egg yolks in a bowl. Pour the just-boiled milk mixture onto the yolks and whisk together well.

Pour the mixture back into the saucepan and continue to cook on a low heat until thickened (but not as thick as a crème anglaise). Remove from the heat and stir in the dulce de leche chocolate, whisking well to incorporate. Pour into a piping bag and cool until needed.

Cut out 8-cm rounds from the cooled puff pastry. Pipe balls of ganache around half of the pastry rounds and alternate with raspberries. Top with another round of pastry. Decorate with finely chopped pistachio nuts.

Frangipane

Frangipane is an almond cream or paste made of eggs, butter, almonds and sugar. It is rich and sweet, making it a perfect combination with buttery puff pastry or the filling for an apricot tart. The method for making it can be applied to other varieties of nuts (pistachios, pecans, etc.) too, which will expand the types of dishes you can experiment with.

1 Put 100g softened butter and 100g caster sugar in the bowl of a stand mixer and beat until creamy and pale.

2 Add 2 medium eggs, one at a time, and beat in.

3 Add 130g ground almonds.

4

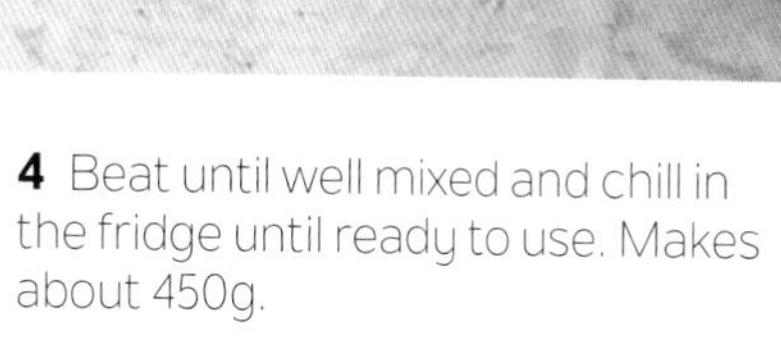

4 Beat until well mixed and chill in the fridge until ready to use. Makes about 450g.

SERVES ABOUT 8

500ml water
300g caster sugar
1 vanilla pod, split lengthways
2 star anise
4 large Williams pears, peeled and cored
½ quantity Rough Puff Pastry
(see pages 134–137)
Frangipane (see pages 182–183)
2 egg yolks, lightly beaten

Pear dartois

Bring the water, sugar and spices to the boil in a saucepan. Add the pears and poach gently for 8–10 minutes, until cooked but still firm. Leave to cool in the syrup until needed.

Preheat the oven to 180°C/350°F/Gas 4.

Roll out the pastry to about 5mm thick and cut into 2 long strips. Place one strip on a baking tray and pierce with a fork at intervals, leaving a 1-cm clear border. Spread or pipe the Frangipane along the middle of the pastry, to come as far as the border.

Drain the pears well, cut each in half and place cut-side down on the Frangipane. Take the second strip of pastry and fold gently in half lengthways, without the 2 sides sticking together. Slice through the fold at intervals, without cutting all the way to the edges (or use a lattice cutter to do this). Open out the strip and brush the edges with egg yolk.

Place the lattice strip on top of the base and gently seal the pastry edges together all the way around. Brush with the remaining egg yolk and bake for 20–25 minutes, until golden and crispy. Make sure you check the base to see if it's cooked and golden brown, too. Leave to cool and serve warm.

Individual dartois also look very impressive.

MAKES 1 LARGE TART

Rough Puff Pastry (see pages 134–137)
15 medium fresh apricots, halved and pitted

PISTACHIO CREAM

140g shelled and skinned unsalted pistachios
100g unsalted butter, diced
100g caster sugar
2 medium eggs

TO FINISH

Melted butter, for brushing
Caster sugar, for sprinkling

Apricot tart

For the pistachio cream, blitz the pistachios to a powder. Beat the butter and sugar together in a bowl until creamy. Add the eggs, one at a time, then fold in the pistachio powder and chill in the fridge.

Preheat the oven to 180°C/350°F/Gas 4. Line a large baking tray with baking parchment.

Roll out the pastry to a circle (or a freeform shape of your choice) about 3mm thick and place on the baking tray. Pierce the pastry at intervals with a fork, then pipe a thin layer of pistachio cream over the surface, leaving a 2-cm border around the edges.

Cut the apricots into thick slices and arrange in neat overlapping layers to cover the pistachio mixture. Fold in the edges of the pastry, then brush all over with melted butter and sprinkle with sugar. Bake for 20–25 minutes, until cooked. Serve with candied pistachios and vanilla ice cream.

SERVES 4

300g raspberries, plus extra to serve
40g caster sugar
20ml lemon juice
Rough Puff Pastry (see pages 134–137)
1 egg yolk, lightly beaten
Demerara sugar, for sprinkling

HAZELNUT CREAM

200g butter, softened
200g caster sugar
4 eggs
100g plain flour
200g ground, roasted hazelnuts

Hazelnut pithiviers

Preheat the oven to 180°C/350°F/Gas 4.

Put the raspberries, sugar and lemon juice in a blender and blend until smooth. Strain the purée through a sieve into a bowl and set aside.

For the hazelnut cream, beat the butter and sugar together in a large bowl, using a wooden spoon, until light and fluffy. Add the eggs, one at a time, beating well between each addition. Sift the flour and ground hazelnuts together, then fold them into the mixture. It should be a thick paste.

Roll out the pastry to 3mm thick. Cut out 4 circles, about 14cm in diameter, then another 4 that are 10cm in diameter. Make a hole in the centre of each larger circle. Spoon about 100g of the hazelnut cream into the centre of each smaller circle, leaving a 1-cm border. Brush the border of the pastry with egg yolk, then drape the larger circle of pastry over the top, crimping the edges with a fork to seal. Using the back of a butter knife, score any pattern you like in the pastry lids. Roll up a small piece of baking parchment and insert it in the hole in the lid to let the steam escape.

Brush the tops of the pastry with egg yolk, then sprinkle with some Demerara sugar. Bake for 25–30 minutes, until the pastry is golden brown. Serve with the raspberry purée and fresh raspberries.

SERVES 4–6

200g butter, softened
150g caster sugar
2 pinches of ground cinnamon
300g cooking apples, peeled, cored and thickly sliced
150g blackberries
2 eggs
120g ground almonds

Apple and blackberry bake

Preheat the oven to 160°C/325°F/Gas 3.

Press 80g of the soft butter evenly out over the base of a pie dish, about 22cm square. Pour 60g of the sugar and the ground cinnamon over the butter to cover and give it a light shake to create an even layer.

Arrange the apple slices in an overlapping layer to cover the base. Sprinkle the blackberries over the apples and set aside.

Beat the remaining 120g soft butter and the remaining 90g sugar together until pale and creamy. Beat in the eggs, one at a time. Mix in the ground almonds, then spread the mixture over the apple and berries.

Bake for 55–60 minutes. Leave to sit for 10 minutes before serving with a scoop of vanilla ice cream.

SERVES 6

400g shortcrust pastry
1 punnet of red raspberries
1 punnet of golden raspberries
Pistachio Cream (see page 187)
Freshly grated pistachios, for sprinkling
Clotted cream, to serve

Raspberry and pistachio Bakewell tart

Preheat the oven to 190°C/375°F/Gas 5.

Roll out the shortcrust pastry until big enough to line a 23-cm tart tin and use to line the tin. Line with baking parchment and fill with baking beans or uncooked rice, then blind bake for 15 minutes, until golden.

Remove the baking beans and parchment, return the pastry case to the oven and cook for a further 5 minutes. Remove from the oven and spread the red raspberries and half the golden raspberries onto the base.

Pipe the Pistachio Cream evenly over the top, return to the oven and bake for 20–25 minutes, until risen and golden. Sprinkle the freshly grated pistachios on top and serve with clotted cream and the remaining golden raspberries.

Sabayon

This is an easy sauce that is similar to hollandaise. Egg yolks, sugar and a liquid (alcohol or reduced-fruit poaching liquor) are whisked well over heat to produce a light and airy sauce – perfect to fold into whipped cream and cover fresh fruit, and then caramelised under a hot grill. But as you will find here, there are also other ways to use a sabayon.

1 Put 80g caster sugar, 5 egg yolks and 100ml sweet wine or flavoured eau-de-vie in a heatproof bowl set over a pan of barely simmering water on a low heat.

2 Whisk together using a balloon whisk.

3 Keep whisking over the heat until it thickens, doubles in volume and turns pale. When you lift up the whisk it should leave behind a ribbon trail.

4 Take off the heat and leave to cool to room temperature, then fold in 300g lightly whipped double cream. Makes about 500g.

SERVES 6–8

200ml water
100g caster sugar
1 vanilla pod, split lengthways
300g semi-dried apricots
4–6 fresh apricots, pitted
Sabayon (see pages 192–193)
Granola with dried apricots, to decorate

Frozen apricot parfaits

Heat the water, sugar and vanilla together in a pan to make a syrup. Add the semi-dried apricots, bring to the boil and boil for 2 minutes, then set aside to cool. When cool, remove the apricots and roughly chop.

Blitz the fresh apricots to a purée in a blender.

Spoon enough Sabayon into 6–8 moulds about 6cm in diameter and 5cm deep to come halfway up, then spoon some of the cooked, chopped apricots into the middle of each. Fill the moulds with more sabayon and freeze until set.

Serve the parfaits with the apricot purée and some granola.

SERVES 4

2 quinces, peeled, cored and quartered
6 egg yolks
90g caster sugar
125ml whipping cream, semi whipped
100g roasted and peeled chestnuts

POACHING LIQUID

500ml Madeira
250ml water
200g caster sugar
1 cinnamon stick
2 cloves
1 red chilli, split lengthways
3 cardamom pods, crushed

Poached quince and chestnut sabayon

Put all the poaching liquid ingredients into a large saucepan and slowly bring to a simmer. Add the quince quarters to the simmering liquid and poach until tender, about 30–40 minutes. Leave to cool in the syrup, then strain the syrup and set aside 125ml.

Put the egg yolks into a heatproof bowl with the sugar and the 125ml cooled poaching liquor and whisk over a pan of simmering water until really thick and light, about 8 minutes. Take off the heat and fold in the semi-whipped cream.

Put the quince pieces and the roasted chestnuts into a shallow baking dish and cover with the sabayon sauce. Put the whole dish under a hot grill and colour the top evenly, then serve warm.

SERVES 8–10

3 eggs, plus 4 egg yolks
125g caster sugar
370g good-quality dark chocolate, broken into pieces
250g butter

HAZELNUT SABLÉS

340g plain flour
120g icing sugar
1 tsp salt
270g chilled unsalted butter, cubed
70g skinned, roasted hazelnuts, ground to a powder
1 large egg yolk

Dense baked chocolate sabayon with hazelnut sablés

For the hazelnut sablés, sift the flour, icing sugar and salt together into a large bowl. Make a well in the centre and add the cubed butter to the well. Using your fingertips, quickly work the butter into the flour mixture until almost incorporated. Add the hazelnuts and egg yolk and gently knead until the dough comes together. Wrap the dough in cling film and leave to rest in the fridge for 30 minutes.

Preheat the oven to 160°C/325°F/Gas 3.

Roll the dough out between 2 pieces of baking parchment until 4mm thick. Transfer to a baking tray and bake for 20 minutes, until just browned on the bottom. Cut into the shapes you want while still warm. Reduce the oven temperature to 135°C/275°F/Gas 1.

Make a sabayon using the whole eggs, egg yolks and sugar (see pages 192–193). Meanwhile, melt the chocolate and butter together in a heatproof bowl set over a pan of barely simmering water. Fold the melted chocolate mixture into the sabayon and pour into 8–10 x 8-cm moulds. Bake for 10–12 minutes, then serve with the hazelnut sablés.

SERVES 4

12 fresh green almonds in the shell, plus extra to serve
3 apricots
12 strawberries
1 punnet of golden raspberries
Sabayon (see pages 192–193)
1 lime (optional)

Summer fruits, fresh almonds and sabayon

Place the almonds, apricots, strawberries and raspberries in a serving dish. Top with the Sabayon and glaze very quickly with a kitchen blowtorch, or under a very hot grill. Grate some fresh almonds and lime zest, if using, over the top, then serve.

Caramel

Making caramel at home is a great way to elevate your desserts to another level. You can use it to make sugar decorations to finish a dessert, or as the base for a caramel sauce, among many others. Understanding the process of making caramel will help you become more confident, and then, more creative. This is my go-to caramel because it's fool-proof and there's no risk of crystallising.

1 Put 200g caster sugar in a clean, heavy-based pan without any water on a medium-high heat, and heat until it begins to caramelise. You can stir it to get the colour even, but make sure the spoon is dry.

2 When it starts to melt into a light golden caramel, turn down the heat so it doesn't burn.

3 You are aiming for a smooth, golden caramel.

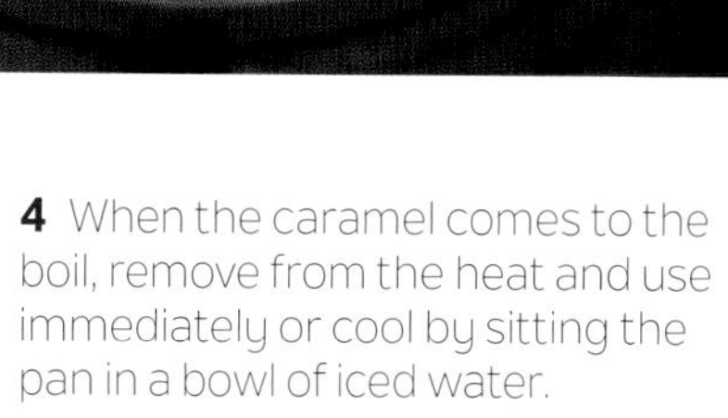

4 When the caramel comes to the boil, remove from the heat and use immediately or cool by sitting the pan in a bowl of iced water.

MAKES AT LEAST 30,
FOR DECORATION

200g fondant paste
50g liquid glucose
100g milk chocolate pieces

Pulled caramel thins

These caramel decorations look stunning and are actually easier to make than you think!

Have ready a sink or large bowl of ice-cold water. Bring the fondant paste and glucose to the boil in a heavy-based saucepan, and cook to 121°C. Stop the cooking by dipping the base of the pan into the ice-cold water. Add the chocolate and mix in, then pour out onto a silicone mat. Leave to cool a little, then pull the sheets of sugar until very thin to create decorative shapes.

MAKES 20

325g caster sugar
50g honey
125g liquid glucose
60ml water
15g bicarbonate of soda
300g good-quality dark chocolate, broken into pieces (60% cocoa solids)

Chocolate-dipped honeycomb

Line a deep baking tray with baking parchment.

Put the sugar, honey, glucose and water into a heavy-based saucepan. Bring up to 151°C, then immediately remove from the heat and leave for 10 seconds to settle.

Carefully whisk in the bicarbonate of soda and quickly pour the mixture into the lined tray. Leave to cool before cutting into pieces.

Melt the chocolate in a heatproof bowl set over a pan of barely simmering water, then dip the cooled honeycomb pieces in the chocolate and leave on a sheet of baking parchment until the chocolate has set.

SERVES 5–6

50ml vegetable oil
120g popping corn
1 tsp sea salt
200g caster sugar
Butter, for greasing

ICE CREAM

400ml whole milk
400ml double cream
1 vanilla pod, split lengthways
and seeds scraped
120g egg yolks (about 6 eggs)
200g caster sugar
10g sea salt (optional)

PEANUT AND POPCORN PRALINE

200g caster sugar
100g roasted peanuts
20g popped popcorn

Popcorn caramel ice cream

Heat the oil and popping corn in a large saucepan fitted with a lid on a medium heat and shake until all the kernels have popped. Remove the lid and sprinkle the salt over the popcorn.

Make a caramel with the caster sugar (see pages 200–201), add the popcorn, then tip onto a buttered, baking parchment-lined tray to cool. Set some aside for serving and put the rest into a bowl.

For the ice cream, heat the milk, cream and vanilla pod and seeds until just boiling, then remove from the heat. Whisk the egg yolks and sugar in a bowl until pale, then slowly whisk in the cream and milk mixture. Pour back into the pan and cook on a low heat until slightly thickened, then strain through a sieve onto the popcorn in the bowl. Mix, cover with cling film and leave to infuse overnight in the fridge.

The next day, strain the mixture, pressing down on the popcorn to extract all the creamy mixture. Taste and add the salt, if needed. Churn in an ice-cream machine until set.

For the peanut and popcorn praline, make a dry caramel with half the sugar (see pages 200–201), add the roasted peanuts and pour out on a buttered, baking parchment-lined tray. Do the same with the remaining sugar and popcorn, and leave to cool. Break into pieces when set.

Serve the ice cream with the reserved popcorn and little pieces of peanut and popcorn praline.

SERVES 6

6 Braeburn apples
2 tbsp plain flour
6 strips of Rough Puff Pastry (see pages 134–137), each 1 x 30cm
4 tbsp salted butter, softened
100g Demerara sugar

SAUCE

300g granulated sugar
150ml water
100ml Calvados
40g salted butter
150ml double cream

Baked apples with Calvados caramel sauce

Peel and core the apples, then dust with the flour. Take a strip of pastry and wrap it horizontally around the outside of an apple, overlapping the layers slightly so that the finished result resembles a beehive. Repeat with the remaining pastry strips and apples, then chill in the fridge.

Preheat the oven to 180°C/350°F/Gas 4. Line a baking tray with baking parchment.

Brush the chilled apples with the softened butter then sprinkle liberally with the Demerara sugar, covering the entire apple. Put the apples onto the lined baking tray and bake for about 25 minutes, until the pastry and apples are cooked.

Meanwhile, for the sauce, put the granulated sugar and water in a saucepan. Heat to dissolve the sugar, then cook until it has reached a nice caramel colour. Take off the heat and add the Calvados, butter and cream. Put back on the heat and gently whisk everything back together into a rich caramel sauce.

Serve the apples with the sauce and a scoop of vanilla ice cream.

MAKES ABOUT 20

60g caster sugar
60g liquid glucose

Caramel tuiles

Preheat the oven to 180°C/350°F/Gas 4.

Cook the sugar and glucose in a heavy-based pan to make a caramel (see pages 200–201). Pour onto a silicone mat to cool and set completely. Once set, break it into small pieces, place in a blender and blitz to a very fine powder.

Use a small sieve to dust a layer about 1mm thick of the powder mixture onto a silicone mat. Separate out circles of the powder with a round cookie cutter. This will help the caramel to melt into circles in the oven. Place in the oven and cook until completely melted, 4–5 minutes. Remove and leave to set and firm up before sliding a thin spatula under the circles gently to remove them from the mat.

These tuiles look really stunning! You can also add nuts to the caramel.

Basics

Mushroom duxelles

2 banana shallots, finely chopped
2 tbsp butter
1 thyme sprig
2 fresh bay leaves
500g button mushrooms,
very finely chopped
200ml double cream
Salt and freshly ground black pepper

Sweat the shallots in the butter and add the thyme and bay. Add the mushrooms, season well and sweat for 5 minutes. Add the cream and cook out until dry. Set aside.

Lobster bisque

6 lobster heads (see pages 68–69)
Olive oil, for cooking
1 small fennel bulb
1 onion
2 carrots
3 celery stalks
1 tbsp tomato paste
100g plain flour
200ml brandy
100ml white wine
600ml Fish Stock (see opposite)
2 fresh or dried bay leaves
Bunch of basil stalks
4 tomatoes, cut into chunks
Cream (optional)

Crush or chop the lobster heads into pieces. Heat a little olive oil in a large saucepan. Add the vegetables and colour gently. Add the lobster pieces and cook for 3–4 minutes. Add the tomato paste and cook for 2 minutes, then stir in the flour and cook out. Add the alcohol and reduce by half. Add the Fish Stock, bay leaves, basil and tomatoes and bring to the boil. Cook on a gentle simmer for 1 hour, skimming off any scum that forms on the surface. Pass through a sieve, then pour back into a pan and reduce the bisque to the required consistency. Finish with a little cream, if needed.

Lobster stock

400g lobster shells and carcass
(see pages 68–69), crushed
1 celery stalk
1 small onion, halved
2 lemon thyme sprigs
2 fresh or dried bay leaves
Zest of ½ lemon

Put the lobster shells and carcass in a large saucepan and add the remaining ingredients. Cover with water, bring to the boil and simmer for 20 minutes. Strain and cool.

Vegetable stock

2 onions, peeled
2 small carrots, peeled
1 small leek (white part), washed
2 celery stalks
1.5 litres water

Cut the vegetables into large chunks and place in a deep stockpot. Pour on the water to cover and bring to the boil. Lower the heat and simmer gently for about 45 minutes. Pass the stock through a conical sieve into a bowl and allow to cool. Refrigerate for up to 3–4 days until ready to use, or freeze in convenient batches.

NOTE I tend to add whatever vegetable trimmings I may have to hand to this basic recipe, such as ripe tomatoes or even just the skins, as well as herb stalks.

Fish stock

1kg white fish bones and trimmings (from sea bass, sole, turbot, etc.)
50ml olive oil
1 leek (white part), washed and cut into chunks
1 onion, roughly chopped
2 celery stalks, roughly chopped
3 garlic cloves, halved
150ml dry white wine
1.5 litres water
1 heaped tsp white peppercorns
Bouquet Garni (see below)

Rinse the fish bones and trimmings and drain in a colander. Heat the olive oil in a stockpot and add the vegetables and garlic. Sweat on a medium heat for a few minutes, without colouring. Add the fish bones and trimmings and cook gently for 2–3 minutes. Pour in the wine and let bubble to reduce by two-thirds. Now pour in the water to cover everything and add the peppercorns and bouquet garni. Bring to the boil, skim off any scum from the surface and turn down to a gentle simmer. Cook for about 20 minutes, skimming as necessary. Pass the stock through a conical sieve into a bowl and allow to cool. Refrigerate for up to 2 days until ready to use, or freeze in convenient batches.

Chicken stock

1kg chicken carcasses or wings
2 onions, quartered
3 celery stalks, cut into large chunks
1 leek (white part), washed and cut into chunks
2 litres water
Bouquet Garni (see below)

Put the chicken bones or wings into a stockpot with the vegetables. Pour on the water to cover and bring to the boil. Skim off any scum from the surface, add the bouquet garni and turn down to a gentle simmer. Cook for 1 hour, skimming as necessary; do not allow to boil. Pass the stock through a conical sieve into a bowl and allow to cool. Refrigerate for up to 3–4 days until ready to use, or freeze in convenient batches.

BOUQUET GARNI I use a few thyme sprigs, a few parsley stalks, a bay leaf and the green part of the leek, tied together with kitchen string.

Mushroom broth

4 shallots, sliced
2 tbsp olive oil
2 garlic cloves, chopped
2 fresh or dried bay leaves
1 thyme sprig
1kg button mushrooms, sliced
100ml Madeira

Sweat the shallots in the olive oil, then add the garlic, bay and thyme. Add the mushrooms and cook until lightly coloured. Deglaze with the Madeira. Add water to just cover the mushrooms and simmer gently for 1 hour, uncovered. Strain and chill until ready to use.

MUSHROOM AND MARMITE BROTH Start the recipe as above, but after the mushrooms have coloured, add 3–4 tbsp Marmite to the pan. Cook for 5 minutes before deglazing with the Madeira and continuing with the recipe.

Beef or lamb stock

1kg beef or lamb bones
Olive oil, for cooking
2 carrots
1 onion
2 celery stalks
1 leek, halved
Bouquet garni made from 3 thyme sprigs, 2 fresh or dried bay leaves and 2 rosemary sprigs
2 litres water

Preheat the oven to 180°C/350°F/Gas 4.

Put the bones in a roasting tray and roast until golden brown. Heat a stockpot and add a little olive oil. Add the vegetables and cook to colour them. Add the roasted bones, bouquet garni and water and bring to the boil. Simmer for 1–2 hours. Strain before using, and then boil to reduce it if you need a more intense stock.

Lemon curd

1 whole egg, plus 2 medium egg yolks
80g caster sugar
Juice of 2 lemons
50g butter

Whisk the egg and yolks, sugar and lemon juice together in a pan on a low heat, or in a heatproof bowl set over a pan of simmering water, whisking continuously until very thick (ribbon stage). Cool slightly then whisk in the butter and refrigerate until needed.

Stock syrup

100g caster sugar
100ml water

Put the sugar and water into a saucepan and heat until the sugar has dissolved and you have a syrup.

Chelsea bun fillings

Praline and caramel
200g caster sugar
200g roasted, skinned hazelnuts
300g praline paste (or Nutella)

Melt the sugar in a saucepan on a medium heat and cook until it has reached a light caramel colour, then add the hazelnuts, coating them quickly in the caramel. Butter a piece of baking parchment and use to line a baking tray. Pour the nut mixture onto the tray and spread them out in a single layer. Leave to cool, then crush the nuts up.

Spread the praline paste over the rolled out rectangle of Chelsea bun dough, scatter the crushed hazelnut caramel over the paste before rolling up the dough.

Cinnamon, rum and sultanas
250ml rum
150g sultanas
200g salted butter, at room temperature
200g granulated sugar
1 tbsp ground cinnamon

Bring the rum to the boil in a pan and remove from the heat. Add the sultanas and leave to soak for 5 minutes. Mix the butter, sugar and cinnamon together in a large bowl. Drain the sultanas and fold into the butter mixture.

Spread the filling over the rolled out rectangle of Chelsea bun dough and then roll it up.

Crème pâtissière

250ml milk
1 vanilla pod, split lengthways
65g caster sugar
3 medium egg yolks
30g plain flour

Pour the milk into a heavy-based saucepan with the vanilla, bring to the boil, then remove from the heat. In a bowl, mix the sugar, egg yolks and flour together. Pour the hot milk onto the egg mixture and whisk, then pour back into the pan and cook until thick. Strain into a clean bowl, cover with a layer of cling film to prevent a skin from forming and leave to cool.

GLOSSARY

ACIDULATED WATER
Water to which an acid like lemon juice or vinegar has been added. Cut fruit or vegetables are submerged in it to prevent oxidisation and browning.

AGNOLOTTI
Little filled pasta parcels.

BAIN MARIE
To cook something surrounded by water for gentle and even heating.

BLANCHING
To cook food, usually vegetables, very briefly in boiling water to partially cook them or to make it easier to remove the skin. The blanched vegetables are often refreshed in ice-cold water to preserve the colour and/or stop the cooking process.

BLIND BAKING
To bake a pastry base, before filling it. This is often done if the filling doesn't need cooking. The pastry base is usually weighted down with baking beans (or raw rice) to stop the pastry from puffing up in the oven.

BOUQUET GARNI
A bundle of herbs tied together and used to infuse stocks, soups, etc.

CARTOUCHE
A round of paper placed directly on the contents of a saucepan to stop them drying out, or to keep them submerged.

CLARIFIED BUTTER
The clear liquid obtained when butter is melted and cooked until it breaks down into parts.

CROQUETTES
Little balls of mixture coated in breadcrumbs and fried until crispy on the outside and soft inside.

DARTOIS
Puff pastry parcel filled with almond cream.

DEGLAZING
To pour liquid such as wine into a hot pan where ingredients have been fried in order to scrape up and incorporate the flavoursome bits stuck to the pan.

DUXELLES
A base of very finely chopped mushrooms.

GANACHE
A base made from chocolate and cream and used in many desserts.

GREMOLATA
An Italian seasoning made from very finely chopped herbs (usually parsley), lemon zest and garlic.

JULIENNE
To cut vegetables into thin matchstick shapes.

LIQUOR
The liquid that's left after food has been poached or cooked in it.

MALTAISE
Hollandaise sauce flavoured with blood orange.

ORECCHIETTE
Small pasta pieces that resemble 'little ears', from which the Italian name originates.

PALMIERS
French biscuits made from puff pastry and shaped into distinctive flat, symmetrical swirls.

PARFAIT
A creamy frozen dessert.

PASSING
To press a paste or purée through a fine-mesh sieve.

PIEROGI
Polish dumplings with a filling.

PITHIVIERS
Large, circular puff pastry tart with a distinctive swirly pattern scored in the top and often filled with almond cream.

PRALINE
A confection usually consisting of nuts and caramelised sugar.

PROVING
To leave bread dough to rest and rise before baking in order for the yeast to ferment.

QUENELLE
An oval or egg shape created by shaping a mousse or cream between 2 spoons.

ROUX
A base made from cooked flour and butter which is then added to liquid to thicken it.

REDUCING
To cook a liquid on a high heat so as to evaporate some of it and intensify the flavour.

RIBBON STAGE
When a mixture is whisked to the point that the whisk, when lifted, leaves a trail like a ribbon on the surface of the mixture.

ROUX
A base of flour and butter, cooked together and used to thicken sauces.

SABLÉ
A delicate French biscuit similar to shortbread.

SPATCHCOCKING
To flatten a chicken or other poultry for even cooking, usually by removing the backbone.

TARTE FINE
A tart made from a thin base of (usually) puff pastry topped with thinly sliced fruit.

TARTIFLETTE
A dish from the French Alps traditionally made with cheese, potatoes, lardons and onions.

TEMPURA
Japanese dish of battered and fried vegetables, prawns, etc.

TORTELLINI
Little filled pasta parcels that are said to resemble navels.

TUILE
A very thin biscuit/wafer that can be shaped and moulded when warm.

INDEX

See also Glossary on pages 214-15

The 20 key skills are listed in *italics*

Publishing Director: **Sarah Lavelle**
Creative Director: **Helen Lewis**
Senior Editor: **Céline Hughes**
Designers: **Lucy Gowans, Katherine Keeble**
Photographer: **Cristian Barnett**
Prop Stylist: **Polly Webb-Wilson**
Assistant Food Stylist: **Renee Miller**
Production Controller: **Tom Moore**
Production Manager: **Vincent Smith**

First published in 2016 by
Quadrille Publishing Limited
Pentagon House
52–54 Southwark Street
London SE1 1UN
www.quadrille.co.uk

Quadrille is an imprint of Hardie Grant
www.hardiegrant.com.au

Cataloguing in Publication Data: a catalogue record for this book is available from the British Library.

ISBN: 978 184949 764 0

Printed in China

Acknowledgements

Thanks to Renee Miller, Laura Cadiere, Cristian Barnett, Polly Webb-Wilson, Lucy Gowans, Rosemary Scoular and everyone at Quadrille who made this book possible.